The Blasphemy Trial of Charles B. Reynolds

Morristown, New Jersey
May 19-20, 1887

Craig A. Leisy

The Blasphemy Trial of Charles B. Reynolds
Morristown, New Jersey
May 19-20, 1887

ISBN Number: 978-1-60571-115-7

Printed in the United States of America

Dedication

This book is dedicated to my mother Phyllis Leisy who passed along her interest in history to me and has encouraged me to write about it.

Acknowledgements

I am indebted to many people for their valuable assistance in researching this book. I would especially like to thank the following: Stephanie Gabelmann at the Boonton Holmes Public Library; Marilyn Stearns and Christine Jochem at the North Jersey History Center; David Mitros at the Morris County Heritage Commission; Tom O'Malley and Bette Epstein at the New Jersey State Library; Peter Chimenti at the Seventh-day Adventist Church; Nick Kersten at the Seventh Day Baptist Church; Mary Schaff at the Washington State Library; and Bonnie Lange at *The Truth Seeker*.

Table of Contents

Introduction

On May 19, 1887, ex-minister Charles B. Reynolds was placed on trial by the State of New Jersey charged with blasphemy. It was the first blasphemy trial in that state and the first in the United States in more than 50 years. Reynolds stood accused of distributing a pamphlet ridiculing both the Christian God and the Bible during freethought lectures he delivered in Boonton and Morristown.

Attorney Col. Robert G. Ingersoll, who commanded a regiment of Illinois volunteer cavalry during the Civil War, defended Reynolds in a trial that was reported on by *The New York Times* and received national attention. Col. Ingersoll, an agnostic, was a popular lecturer and author and was widely known as a strong proponent for separation between church and state. Both Col. Ingersoll and Reynolds were officers of the American Secular Union which was in the forefront of the secular movement sweeping across the nation.

This is the story of the famous blasphemy trial told in the words of Reynolds, Col Ingersoll and their contemporaries. The trial is viewed in the context of the post-Civil War era of rapid social change caused by industrialization, immigration and westward expansion.

Some historians see a similarity between the Reynolds blasphemy trial in 1887 and the Scopes trial in 1925 for teaching evolution in the public schools. The trials represented the high water marks of the secular movement in the nineteenth and twentieth centuries respectively.

The Reynolds blasphemy trial was a direct consequence of the conflict between religion and the secular movement. The secular movement has since passed into history but the effects of the trial on free speech are still with us. The Reynolds blasphemy trial, though largely forgotten now, helped bring about the modern secular society we live in. Many issues raised by the trial are still being debated today.

Craig Leisy
Seattle, Washington
2011

Early Life

Little is known about the early life of Charles B. Reynolds. He was probably born in New York City on August 5, 1832. Burial records indicate that he lived 64 years, 11 months, and 26 days and died on July 31, 1896 in the Fremont neighborhood of Seattle, Washington.[1] The only biographical information on the early life of Charles is provided by Samuel Putnam in his short histories of famous freethinkers published near the end of the nineteenth century.[2] Putnam reported that the parents of Charles immigrated from Somershire [sic], England to the United States and lived in the city of New York.[3] There is a family story that Charles' parents were

---

[1] Seattle Genealogical Society. *Mt. Pleasant Cemetery Seattle, WA: Information taken from tombstones, Sexton's records and Marie Freeman's files 1861-1972* Vol. 2 M-Z Seattle, WA (1999). The entry for Reynolds states, "Reynolds, C. B., b. New York, d. 31Jul1896 Fremont, WA, funeral: 1Aug 1896, age: 64y 11m 26d, kin: son-in-law A. D. Grow, t/s." However, the Death Certificate for Charles B. Reynolds indicates his age as 63 years and this information was most likely obtained from his spouse who survived him. The Death Certificate shows his date of death as July 31, 1896 and his cause of death as meningitis.

[2] Samuel P. Putnam. *400 Years of Freethought* New York: The Truth Seeker Company (1894), pp. 792-794. Putnam was a close associate of Reynolds in the American Secular Union at the time of the celebrated blasphemy trial. Putnam was secretary and Reynolds chaired the executive committee of the American Secular Union. Both were traveling lecturers. The biographical sketch of Reynolds contained in George E. MacDonald *Fifty Years of Freethought* 2 vols. New York: Arno Press & *The New York Times* (1972) [reprint of 1929 ed.], Vol. 2, pp. 130-131 clearly borrows from Putnam's work.

[3] There is no town, city or county in England named "Somershire." According to the National Archives of the United Kingdom, "Somershire is likely to be the county of Somerset, sometimes called Somersetshire" [e-mail communication on November 15, 2008]. Judy Reynolds, daughter of Elaine Davis and George R. Reynolds,

members of an acting troupe.[4] According to Putnam, the mother of Charles died during childbirth and his father died before Charles was five years old. Charles had no known relatives living in the United States and he was presumably orphaned.

There is no record of Charles B. Reynolds in the U.S. Census until 1870 when he is shown as aged 37 years and residing with his wife and three children in the town of Parma in the state of New York.[5] In that census, his occupation is given as "minister of gospel." By 1868, Charles had become a minister affiliated with the First Day Adventist Church but he joined the Seventh-day Adventist Church the following year.[6] The periodical

---

eldest grandson of Charles B. Reynolds, learned about him from her father and also relates that his parents immigrated to the U.S. from England. U. S. Census records and the Death Certificate for Charles Reynolds confirm that both of his parents were born in England and that he was born in New York.

[4] Conversation with Michael A. (Mike) Reynolds, his wife Valerie (Val) Sandford, and his mother, Marjorie (Peggie) L. Weiss at her home on October 13, 2008. Peggie, b. Sept. 25, 1924, was the second wife of George R. Reynolds, a grandson of Charles. This is also the recollection of Judy Reynolds, daughter of Elaine Davis, the first wife of George R. Reynolds. Judy related stories she heard from her father.

[5] Reynolds gave his mailing address as Box 104, North Parma, New York in columns he wrote for *The Truth Seeker* when he solicited contributions to support his summer tent lectures. According to Donna Curry, Parma Town Clerk, "Many of our town records were destroyed in a fire some years ago. This included newspapers, and early birth, death and marriage records."

[6] Samuel P. Putnam. *400 Years of Freethought* New York: The Truth Seeker Company (1894), p. 792. According to Peter Chiomenti, Assistant Director of the Office of Archives and Statistics for the General Conference of Seventh-day Adventists (SDA), the SDA church organized in 1863 and membership rolls are not kept in central files. The SDA had no seminary until 1934.

The Seventh-day Adventists began as the Millerite Movement in the early part of the 19th century. However, following the "Great published by the Seventh-day Adventist Church, the *Advent Review and Herald of the Sabbath*, contains two submissions by Charles during 1871.[7] Charles also subscribed to a periodical published by the Seventh Day Baptists, the *Sabbath Recorder*, during 1873-74.[8] There is a family anecdote about how Charles became a minister. When his parents died, Charles was raised by members of their acting troupe since he had no close

---

Disappointment" in 1844 and under the influence of Rachel Oakes Preston, a Seventh Day Baptist, they came to accept Saturday as the Sabbath day. The Seventh-day Adventist sect grew during the "Second Great Awakening," a revival of religion in the U.S. Several other sects were founded during this period including the Mormans. Gary Land. *Historical Dictionary of Seventh-day Adventists* Lanham, MD: The Scarecrow Press (2005).

[7] *Advent Review and Herald of the Sabbath*, Vol. 37, No. 4 "Newfane," regarding a series of meetings in Newfane, New York (near south shore of Lake Ontario in western New York) during Nov. 19-Dec. 27, 1870. It seems that Charles was then affiliated with the Seventh-day Adventist Church of Olcott, New York, about 7 miles to the north, and was reporting on the success of his mission to convert residents there to the Seventh-day Adventist Church. The submission in Vol. 38, No.7 was an obituary for an elderly church member in Lancaster, New York located south of Newfane near Buffalo. Copies of the periodical were provided by Peter Chiomenti, Assistant Director of the Office of Archives and Statistics for the General Conference of Seventh-day Adventists.

[8] *Sabbath Recorder*, Aug. 28, 1873, Vol. 29, Issue 35, p. 149. "C. B. Reynolds, North Parma Pays $2.00 to Vol. 30, No. 50." According to Nick Kersten, Librarian-Historian for the Seventh Day Baptist Historical Society, there were Seventh-day Adventist (SDA) subscribers to the *Sabbath Recorder* published by the Seventh Day Baptists (SDB). He explained that the Adventist movement accepted the Saturday Sabbath following the "Great Disappointment" of 1844 (return of Jesus) and many Seventh Day Baptist members joined the new Seventh-day Adventist sect during the subsequent decades. The Millerite Movement, forerunner of the Seventh-day Adventists, believed that the return of Jesus would occur between March 21, 1843-March 21, 1844. The time was based upon a reading of Daniel 8:14 where 2,300 days was interpreted as 2,300 years. Gary Land. *Historical Dictionary of Seventh-day Adventists* Lanham, MD: The Scarecrow Press (2005).

relatives living in the United States. Charles eventually became an actor in the troupe. While performing in St. Louis (c. 1849), there was a terrible cholera epidemic that killed nearly ten percent of the population. Charles was asked to preside at funeral services because there were not enough clergy. Afterwards, Charles was said to have claimed that preaching paid better than acting so he became a minister.[9]

As late as the 1880 U.S. Census, Charles had given his occupation as "clergyman." However, Charles attended the New York Freethinkers' Convention at the Corinthian Academy of Music in Rochester, New York during September 1883 where he gave a eulogy for D. M. Bennett, the founder of *The Truth Seeker*, a weekly freethinker newspaper.[10] Charles was elected chairman of the Executive Committee of the American Secular Union at the annual convention in Cassadaga, New York during 1884.[11] Charles abandoned his work as a clergyman and, in 1885, he began to tour as a lecturer on secularism.[12] His wife Frances also lectured beginning

---

[9] Judy Reynolds, a great granddaughter of Charles B. Reynolds, recalled this and other family stories related to her by her father, George R. Reynolds. According to her father, Charles traveled the country as a minister but eventually became disillusioned with the ministry and began lecturing on freethought. Unfortunately, Judy could not recall learning from her father about the blasphemy trial discussed in this monograph.
Neither the St. Louis Genealogical Society and Missouri Historical Society could locate any burial records showing Charles B. Reynolds as officiating.
[10] George E. MacDonald. *Fifty Years of Freethought* ,op. cit., p. 140. "D.M. Bennett began its publication in September 1873, at Paris, Illinois, by way of replying to a clergyman who had access to local newspapers, while he had not." The newspaper was moved to the city of New York in 1874.
[11] Samuel P. Putnam. *400 Years of Freethought* New York: The Truth Seeker (1894), p. 792.
[12] MacDonald, *Fifty Years of Freethought* ,op. cit., p. 364.

in 1886.[13] Their children sometimes assisted as well. George E. MacDonald, the long time editor of *The Truth Seeker*, a freethought weekly newspaper, and a close friend, explained why Charles joined the secularist movement.

In the early '80s [Reynolds] began delivering Freethought lectures, having been "converted" by reading the Boston *Investigator* and *The Truth Seeker.*[14]

The *Investigator* and *The Truth Seeker* were popular freethought publications and included the writings of the leading personalities in the American freethought movement of the nineteenth century.

There were a few "freethinker's journals. The Boston *Investigator*, still edited by Horace Seaver, was frankly atheistic. Dr. J. R. Monroe's *Iron-Clad Age* (1855-98) was an agnostic weekly from Indianapolis. The Reverend E. C. Towne's Chicago monthly *Examiner* (1870-1871), which published five numbers, and E.M. McDonald's New York *Truth-Seeker* (1873-current) were radicals. The San Francisco *Universe* (1882-93) was another agnostic.[15]

According to the *New York Times*, Charles Reynolds left the ministry due to the unhistorical nature of the Bible and his rejection of some of its moral teachings.

---

[13] *The Truth Seeker*, Vol. 13, No. 10, February 13, 1886, p. 100. Her first lecture was "Reasons for the Religion of Humanity" at Jobstown, New Jersey.

[14] George E. MacDonald. *Fifty Years of Freethought* ,op. cit., pp. 130-131. And, at p. 364:
"Charles B. Reynolds, ex-Rev., who had made a good impression at the Salamanca Convention of Freethinkers in 1883, now took the field as a lecturer."

[15] See also, Frank Luther Mott. *A History of American Magazines* 4 vols. Vol. III 1865-1885 Cambridge, MA: Harvard University Press (1957), pp. 88-89. E. M. MacDonald, was the long time editor of *The Truth Seeker*.

> It was understood that [Reynolds] had been a Methodist minister: that, finding it impossible to reconcile his mind to some of the historical parts of the Bible and unable to accept it in its entirety as a moral guide, he left the church and set out to proclaim his conclusions.[16]

At the time of the French Revolution and the Age of Reason, irreligious persons were referred to as "rationalists." Eventually, these individuals became known as liberals or secularists but they avoided the label "atheist" as too controversial. The term "secularism" was coined by an English freethinker named George Jacob Holyoake in 1851.[17]

---

[16] "On Trial for Blasphemy: Col. Ingersoll's Defense of Charles B. Reynolds" *New York Times.* May 20, 1887, p. 8. The New York Times erred in stating that Charles was a Methodist minister – possibly because an illustration in his pamphlet, *Blasphemy and the Bible*, depicted him in conflict with the Methodists and Catholics in Boonton, New Jersey."

Two decades earlier, Bishop John W. Colenso, a missionary bishop for the Church of England in Natal, Africa, reached similar conclusions by finding the Books of Moses unhistorical. Colenso was subsequently excommunicated by the Bishop of Capetown for publishing, among other works, his immensely controversial book, *The Pentateuch and Book of Joshua Critically Examined* (1862). The book was strongly condemned by clergy in both England and America. Reynolds was very familiar with Colenso and that book. Reynolds refers to it in his controversial pamphlet, "Blasphemy and the Bible" (1896).

[17] Joss Marsh. *Word Crimes: Blasphemy, Culture and Literature in Nineteenth-Century England* Chicago: The University of Chicago Press (1998), p. 240.

See also, Warren Sylvester Smith. *The London Heretics 1870-1914* New York: Dodd, Mead & Company (1968), p. 30. George Jacob Holyoake, a deist, wished to distinguish between his goal of the separation of church and state and the atheist movement which sought to eliminate religion from society.

"Freethinkers in London at the time were mainly intellectuals. It was Holyoake's aim to appeal to the working men. He coined the word 'secularism' to avoid the negative concept of 'atheism.' " Holyoake himself was prosecuted for blasphemy at Gloucester, England in

During the national meeting of the Unitarians in Syracuse, New York in 1866, a group of non-Christian theists formed the Free Religious Association. Francis Ellingwood Abbott was a leader of the Free Religious Association and he published the *Index* (Toledo, 1870) to advocate for liberal issues in opposition to orthodox religious views. Subsequently, in 1876, this group became the National Liberal League.[18] Later, some members of the National Liberal League broke away and established the American Secular Union. The American Secular Union was formed to focus on the separation of church and state without the distraction of other liberal issues such as obscenity laws and free speech or women's suffrage.[19] The term "freethinker" generally referred to secularists but had been previously used by deists like Thomas Paine in the eighteenth century. George E. MacDonald, the long time editor of *The Truth Seeker*, a popular freethought weekly newspaper, defined "freethought" as follows:

> Freethought is the means by which secularism flourishes and it means human understanding based upon free inquiry and unrestricted argument. The duty of a secularist is to assist mankind in improving conditions of life in this world.[20]

The Secularist movement branched off from the Liberal movement which flourished following the American Civil War. Secularists were more narrowly focused on the subject of the separation between church and state.

1842 while the editor of *The Oracle of Reason* and he served six months in prison.

[18] Philip Hamburger. *Separation of Church and State* Cambridge, MA: Harvard University Press (2002), pp. 288-289.

[19] Ibid., pp. 332-333.

[20] "What is Secularism?" *The Truth Seeker* Vol. 13, No. 10, February 13, 1886, p. 102.

Some historians have concluded that the carnage in that long conflict weakened established religious sentiments in society by undermining belief in a benevolent God. Rapid advances in modern science, which led to industrialization, also challenged dogmatic beliefs and revealed truths of the established religions. For example, Charles Darwin published *Origin of Species* in 1859 which introduced the theory of evolution and reignited the conflict between science and religion which had its origins in the development of science in ancient Greece.[21]

Charles married Frances Cornwell who was 11 years his junior and probably born in 1843. Charles and Frances may have had five children.[22] Records exist for two male and two female children: Etta (Violetta) [b. 1865], Frank (Francis) [b.1867], Clint (Clinton) [b.1869], and Gertrude [b. 1872]. Frances Reynolds was the daughter of John Cornwell and Violette Seamon. She grew up in the town of China in the state of New York. Frances had two sisters (Mary Hellen) and three brothers (John, Sidney, and Albert). It is likely that Violetta, the eldest child of Frances and Charles Reynolds, was named after Violette (Seamon) Cornwell, the mother of Frances Reynolds. Frances was a widow for 38 years and died on March 27, 1934 in Seattle, Washington at the age of 91. The 1910 U. S. Census showed that two of her adult children, Frank B. Reynolds (43) and Gertrude Reynolds (38), were divorced and residing with Frances for a time.

---

[21] The roots of this conflict are ancient and date to the birth of science in the pre-Socratic Greek world. See Craig Leisy. *The Origins of the Conflict between Science and Religion in Ancient Greece* (2011). Some historians mistakenly date the beginning of the conflict to the birth of modern science or the Galileo controversy.

[22] The 1910 U.S. Census shows that Charles and Frances had five children but there is no record of the fifth child.

Nothing at all is known about Etta (Violetta) S. Reynolds, their eldest child. She is shown as attending school at age 15 in the 1880 U.S. Census. The 1890 U.S. Census records were largely destroyed but it is doubtful that she would have still lived at home by that time and it isn't possible to locate her without knowing her married surname.[23]

Frank (Francis) B. Reynolds, the second child, lived most of his adult life in Seattle or Vancouver, Washington and worked as a house painter. He married Beulah A. (Kittle) Reynolds [b. 1890, Washington], a canning factory worker, in 1912.[24] It was his second marriage because the 1910 U. S. Census indicates that he was divorced and living in Seattle with his widowed mother Frances and his divorced sister Gertrude. Frank and Beulah had two children: Richard G. Reynolds [b. 1914, Washington] and Clinton B. Reynolds [b. 1916, Washington]. Clinton was presumably named after Frank's younger brother of the same name.[25] Frank died in 1949 at Woodinville, Washington.[26] Beulah died in 1941 at Seattle, Washington.[27]

---

[23] In the 1910 U.S. Census, Frances Reynolds is shown as having a total of five children but only three were still living. The obituary for Charles B. Reynolds stated, in part, that: "[Reynolds] leaves a wife and one daughter, Mrs. A. D. Grow, residing at Fremont, and four sons and daughters on the Atlantic coast." See "Death of C. B. Reynolds" *Seattle Post-Intelligencer*, Sunday, August 2, 1896, p. 8.

[24] Beulah's parents were George B. [b. 1853, New York] and Nettie M. Kittle [b. 1866, New York].

[25] Obituary for Clinton B. Reynolds that appeared in the *Seattle Post-Intelligencer*, Sunday, October 18, 1970, p. 39:
"Reynolds, Clinton B. of 1874 – 24th E. Husband of Isabelle. Father of David and Ann. At his request no services were held. Rather than flowers the family requests that donations be sent to the A.C.L.U."

[26] Obituary for Frank B. Reynolds, "Services Held for Frank B. Reynolds" *The Bothell Citizen*, Thursday, August 18, 1949, Vol. XL, No. 42, p. 1:

Clint (Clinton) B. Reynolds, the third child of Charles and Frances Reynolds, lived in several states after leaving home in Seattle. The U.S. Census shows that he resided in the following locations: Seattle, Washington (1900), Faulk, South Dakota (1910) and Birch Tree, Missouri (1920). Clint married Fannie J. (Curry) Reynolds [b. 1861, Indiana]. It was her second marriage. Fannie had one son, Milton Odle [b. 1903, South Dakota] from the previous marriage. Fannie's mother was Margaret E. Curry [b. 1826]. Clinton had various occupations including veterinarian work and strawberry farmer.

Gertrude Reynolds, the youngest child of Charles and Frances, married Albert D. Grow [b. 1871, Wisconsin] in 1893. Albert's father, George Grow [b. 1842, Vermont] died on July 29, 1896 at age 54 years and just two days before Gertrude's father, Charles B. Reynolds, died. Both were buried at Mt. Pleasant Cemetery in Seattle – George Grow on July 30, 1896 and Charles Reynolds on August 2, 1896. Gertrude and Albert were

---

"Services were held at the Bothell Funeral Home Tuesday, August 16, at 3 p.m. for Frank B. Reynolds, followed by cremation. He died Sunday. Mr. Reynolds, a retired civil service employee with the Army, had made his home near the Honey Shop, Route 2, Woodinville. Survivors are a brother, C. B. Reynolds, with whom he lived, and two sons, G. R. Reynolds of the Coast Guard ship *Klamath*, stationed on the [Puget] Sound, and C.B. Reynolds, Norfolk, Va. The Rev. E. B. Seymour of the Bothell Free Methodist Church officiated at the services."

[27] Obituary for Beulah Reynolds that appeared in *The Seattle Times*, Tuesday, November 18, 1941, p. 23:

"Reynolds, Beulah of 3661 Woodland Park Ave, aged 52 years, beloved wife of Frank B., mother of George Richard and Clinton B., daughter of Mrs. Henriette Thomas. Member of Martha Washington Lodge, Vancouver, Wash. Funeral services Wednesday, 2:30 p.m. Clark-Rafferty." The same obituary appeared in the *Seattle Post-Intelligencer*, Tuesday, November 18, 1941, p. 22.

divorced sometime before the 1910 U. S. Census which shows Gertrude and her brother Frank both divorced and living with their mother, Frances, in Seattle. Albert Grow subsequently married Elo Grow [b. 1883].

The only grandchildren directly descended from Charles and Frances Reynolds were Frank and Beulah's sons Richard and Clinton who resided in Vancouver, Washington in 1930 at the time of the latest available U.S. Census. Clinton and Fannie Reynolds had no children. Both grandsons are now deceased but they each left two living children of their own – the great grandchildren of Charles and Frances Reynolds.

DIRECT DESCENDENTS OF CHARLES B. REYNOLDS

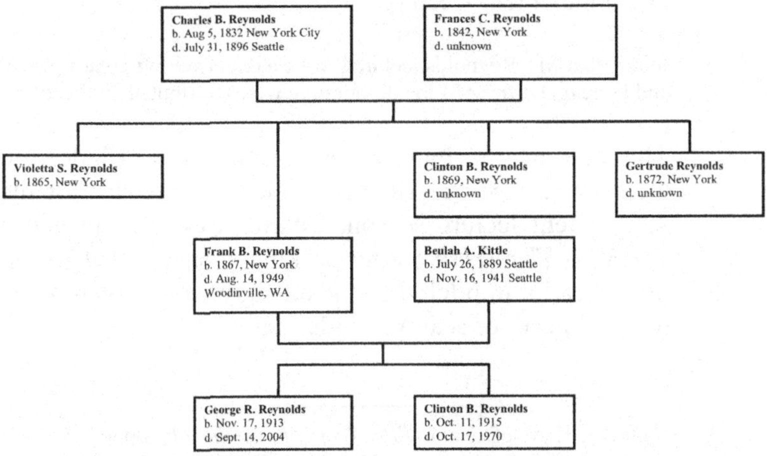

Traveling Lecturer

By 1885, the now ex-Reverend Charles B. Reynolds began work as a traveling lecturer using a large tent because he was unable to rent halls. Usually, church groups in the towns that he visited attempted to stop his lectures by opposing the rental of buildings to him. *The Truth Seeker*, an illustrated weekly freethought newspaper, collected donations from subscribers to purchase the tent.[28] The tent was 50 feet in diameter. A likeness of the tent showing Charles Reynolds, in the foreground, reading an issue of *The Truth Seeker* was published in *The Truth Seeker Annual and Freethinkers' Almanac for 1886.*[29] The initial use of the tent was at Kalamazoo, Michigan on May 30, 1885. The lecture season was generally restricted to the summer months to avoid inclement weather.

> In this tent Mr. Reynolds lectured twice a day, exciting great interest, and large quantities of Liberal literature were distributed and read.[30]

The first tent lecture season eventually concluded on October 1, 1885 in Alliance, Ohio. To prepare for the second tent lecture season, Charles Reynolds placed a notice in *The Truth Seeker* seeking sponsors that would provide a lot to pitch the tent and agree to the loan wood planks to use for seating inside.

---

[28] George E. MacDonald. *Fifty Years of Freethought* ,op. cit., p. 387. "Someone proposed to the ex-Rev. C. B. Reynolds, who had become an effective Freethought lecturer, that he should travel with a tent as a Liberal evangelist. He seized upon the idea, and through the *Truth Seeker* raised the needed funds. William Smith of Geneva, NY, paid for the tent with a contribution of $300."

[29] *The Truth Seeker Annual and Freethinkers' Almanac 1886* New York: *The Truth Seeker*, p. [106]. See illustration on p. 16.

[30] Ibid., pp. 21-22.

I wish to call attention to the fact that I do not desire to pitch the tent where there is already a strong Liberal society able to engage lecturers, but in places where prejudice and bigotry are so great that halls are refused, or where Liberals are so few, or sectarianism so strong, that a course of Liberal lectures in winter is impossible . . . Friends desiring tent effort in their neighborhood are requested to write me [as] soon as possible, so that my route can be positively decided, dates fixed, and all the necessary arrangements fully completed. The tent needs a lot (smooth greensward preferred) not less than 70X75, in a place easy of access, and the use of forty ordinary planks, sixteen feet long. We return them uninjured, as we do not drive nails in them. The tent-master and myself must be provided for during our stay; the tent-master, sleeping in a small tent, requires only use of pillows and quilts. Immediate application is absolutely necessary as we do not wish to waste time and money taking long jumps, and must arrange so as to avoid loss of a single day from the 1st of June to the 1st of November.[31]

The towns visited at the start of the1886 tent lecture season were located in New York and included Williamson (June 10-13), Pultneyville (June 14-15), Marion (June 17) and Palmyra (June 25). Reynolds reported on his tent lectures as he traveled from town to town in a column that appeared regularly in *The Truth Seeker*. In Montezuma, New York, Reynolds anticipated an angry reception by the townspeople but it did not materialize.

Montezuma, N.Y. – I am now quartered at Montezuma. The tent is pitched on the public green…This place will ever be of interest on account of the bitter opposition encountered here by John Remsburg [another freethought lecturer] and myself on our first visit, and the furor of excitement caused immediately after the lectures by the death of Mr. and Mrs. Ross's little child, the Christians declaring the death of the child was the direct vengeance of Jesus, on account of its parents bringing the infidel lecturers to the place.[32]

---

[31] *The Truth Seeker* Vol. 18, No. 15, April 10, 1886, p. 228.
[32] *The Truth Seeker* Vol. 13, No. 29, July 17, 1886, p. 452.

Following Montezuma, Reynolds attended the New York Freethinkers' Association convention in White Sulphur Springs, New York. His next scheduled stop was Boonton, New Jersey where he intended to remain from July 22-August 2, 1886.[33] Reynolds transported the heavy tent on the Lehigh Valley Railroad and he tried to schedule his visits at towns located along the tracks. The 1886 tent season concluded in Camptown, Pennsylvania after repairs were made to damage caused by rioters in Boonton, New Jersey.[34] The following account describes what occurred in Boonton and Morristown, New Jersey during the second "tent campaign."

---

[33] *The Truth Seeker* Vol. 13, No. 27, July 3, 1886, p. 420.

[34] *The Truth Seeker* Vol. 13, No. 41, October 9, 1886, p. 645. By September 19, 1886, "...once more the good cotton cathedral, dedicated to the gospel of humanity, was erect, and looked as neat and pretty as a young maid on her wedding morn."

Arrest for Blasphemy

Charles Reynolds was invited to Boonton, New Jersey by Mrs. A. M. Booth (age 63) and ex-Mayor Edwin Worman (age 68) of the Boonton Secular Union in order to promote secularism. On Monday, July 26, 1886, Reynolds erected his tent near the Crane Brothers store in a lot on Washington Street in Boonton.[35] The lot had been rented for three months by the Booth family for that purpose.[36] There was seating for approximately 200 persons on chairs and plank benches. At one end there was a platform with a stand for the lecturer. Outside the tent was a sign that announced, "Liberal lectures by ex-Rev. C. B. Reynolds – Admission free."[37]

On that first evening the audience was small. Before the lecture, Reynolds distributed some of his writings disparaging of the Catholic Pope and this angered many local church-going townspeople. According to Reynolds,

> My experience is that it is very hard to please the average Jerseyman. I lavished pearls before them and they didn't like it."[38]

A small crowd gathered outside the tent voicing loud protests in an attempt to disrupt the lecture inside. After the first lecture, some persons in the crowd began throwing stones at the tent.

---

[35] *The Iron Era*, July 31, 1886, p. 2.

[36] "The Blasphemy Case: Charles B. Reynolds Telling of His Experience in Boonton" *The New York Times* Nov. 13, 1886, p.8.

[37] "Charged with Blasphemy: Arrest of Ex-Rev. C. B. Reynolds" *The Boonton Weekly Bulletin* Thu., July 29, 1886, p. 1

[38] *The New York Times*, Nov. 13, 1886, op. cit. A reference to biblical scripture at Matthew 7:6 -
Do not give dogs what is holy; and do not throw your pearls before swine, lest they trample them under foot and turn to attack you.

On Tuesday evening, July 27, the tent was full with an estimated 200 persons and, outside, there was a mob of approximately 250 persons. The mob noise caused Reynolds to shorten his lecture. When the tent had cleared it was discovered that two guy ropes supporting the center pole had been cut.[39]

The next morning, on Wednesday, July 28, Reynolds contacted Justice of the Peace Thomas Dennis to file a complaint against five men who he identified as throwing stones: James Neafie (railroad laborer), Josephus E. Dixon (merchant), William Brown (coal dealer), H. G. Randall (bridge tender) and George Hyler (coachman). His complaint charged them with, "inciting to riot, throwing stones at his tent, cutting the ropes, etc." According to Reynolds, "The Justice didn't know enough to draw up a complaint, so I drew it up for him."[40] The men denied the charges.[41] Reynolds also requested that the Mayor provide protection to prevent additional attacks by the mob.

Later, on Wednesday afternoon, a resident of Boonton, New Jersey filed a complaint against Reynolds for violating the state blasphemy law.

Yesterday afternoon Mr. William Brown, coal dealer, and a member of the Reformed Church, went before Justice Van Orden, and made formal charges against C. B. Reynolds, charging him with "publicly blaspheming the Holy name of God by denying and contumaciously reproaching the being and existence of God and of the Scriptures as contained in the books of the old and new Testament," etc.[42]

Marshal Gilmartin served an arrest warrant on Reynolds, at about 7:00 p.m. as he was lighting up the tent for the

---

[39] "Reynolds Arrested for Blasphemy" *The Truth Seeker* Vol. 13, No. 32 August 7, 1886, p. 504.
[40] Ibid.
[41] *The Boonton Weekly Bulletin*, op. cit.
[42] Ibid.

evening lecture, and escorted Reynolds to the station house. Local residents Mrs. A. M. Booth and ex-Mayor Edwin Worman, presumably assisting Reynolds with the tent lectures, accompanied him. A large crowd also assembled. According to Reynolds, "...the mob calling out: 'Tear out his heart,' and advice of a similar nature."[43] At about 7:45 p.m., the charge was read to Reynolds by Justice of the Peace John A. Van Orden.

STATE OF NEW JERSEY,} SS.
MORRIS Co.

Wm. Brown, of said county, on his oath saith that, on the evening of July 27, 1886, he was at a Public meeting, held in a large tent for that purpose, situated on the westerly side of Washington Street, Boonton, N. J., and was addressed by one C. B. Reynolds; and said Reynolds publicly blasphemed the holy name of God, by denying and contumaciously reproaching the being and existence of God and of the Scriptures as contained in the books of the Old and New Testaments by speaking of man in "being made of dust" and saying that used the dust up so he put man to sleep and took a rib out of him and made woman and remarked in a ridiculous manner (who believes such nonsense) and spoke of the Bible, saying of birds and fish were made out of water and said the Bible spoke in another chapter of the same animals being made of clay and remarked (who believes such nonsense) trying to prove the scriptures false and making fun of and ridiculing the Bible and diverse other remarks, therefore the deponent prays that said Reynolds may be arrested and dealt with according to law.

Sworn and subscribed 28th day of July, 1886, before me.
JOHN A. VAN ORDEN, Justice of the Peace[44]

Both Mrs. A. M. Booth and ex-Mayor Edwin Worman offered to pay a bond as security for Reynolds to appear in court on Saturday, July 31, 1886 at 10:00 a.m. Mr. N. S. Kitchel, counsel for the prosecution, objected because Mrs. Booth was a married woman and because Mr.Worman did not own sufficient property. Ultimately,

---

[43] *The New York Times*, Nov. 13, 1886, op. cit.
[44] *The Truth Seeker Annual and Freethinkers' Almanac 1887*, p. 21.

a councilman, John Maxfield, paid the bond in the amount of $300 and Reynolds returned to the tent with his companions.[45]

Afterwards, preparations for the lecture that evening continued. The small audience inside the tent probably included Reynold's wife, Mrs. Frances C. Reynolds, and their two sons.[46] Mr. John Krahmer, a freethinker from New York City, who served as tent master in Boonton, New Jersey, also assisted Reynolds with the lectures. The Booth family, including Mrs. A. M. Booth with five daughters and two sons, were present in the audience. One daughter, Kate Booth (later Mrs. George Gillen of Nutley, New Jersey) subsequently attended the Congress of the American Secular Union in Chickering Hall, New York City during November 11-14, 1886 and was active in the Boonton, New Jersey Secular Union.[47] It is likely that there were other members of the Boonton, New Jersey Secular Union present for the lecture on Wednesday, July 28, including ex-Mayor Edwin Worman. However, according to the local newspaper, *The Boonton Weekly Bulletin*, the audience inside the tent was much smaller than the protesters gathered outside the tent.

---

[45] *The Boonton Weekly Bulletin*, op. cit.

[46] Charles B. Reynolds and Frances C. Reynolds eventually had five sons and daughters. One daughter, Mrs. Albert Grow, and two sons survived him after his death in Seattle, Washington on July 31, 1896. According to his obituary printed in the newspaper and Seattle Genealogical Society records, Charles was buried in Mount Pleasant Cemetery but my wife Vickie and I have conducted searches and are unable to locate his grave marker.

[47] She was likely a member of the Women's Liberal League of Boonton which had several representatives in the courtroom for the blasphemy trial of Reynolds in Morristown, New Jersey during May 19-20, 1887. See "Jersey Law Triumphant: Reynolds Found Guilty of Blasphemy", *The New York Times*, May 21, 1887, p.8.

Reynolds returned to his tent and began to lecture after his bond was paid. According to Reynolds, "Having given bail bonds, I was bound to deliver my lecture that night."[48] *The Boonton Weekly Bulletin* reported on the interrupted lecture that followed.

> As soon as Reynolds left the Station House he went to his tent and began his lecture by calling Wm. Brown an 'ignorant rioter,' and by reading from the Bible to prove the words he was charged with were the statements of Scripture. He said: 'If I was charged with disbelieving the stuff about man being made of dust and the woman from the rib of man, it would be true.' He was proceeding with his lecture, when Marshal Gilmartin appeared upon the scene. 'What," said Reynolds, as the Marshal approached the platform, 'another warrant for me?' [49]

The Marshal announced that the Mayor and the Common Council had directed him to notify Reynolds that the Town of Boonton would not be liable for any damages that might result if he continued his lectures.[50] Reynolds, fearing for the safety of his audience, ended the lecture. According to *The Boonton Weekly Bulletin*, "There was intense excitement on Main Street where the citizens had gathered in great numbers. They were wonderfully aroused and determined to stop the lectures."[51]

Reynolds was forced to make his escape from the tent to avoid violence to him and his audience.

> Threats of lynching, tar and feathers, stoning, and drowning were freely made, and but for the individual and collective bravery of the Booth family, Mr. Reynolds would without doubt have been maltreated personally and thrown into the Morris & Essex canal which ran close by. This family deserves to be remembered.

---

48 *The New York Times*, Nov. 13, 1886, op. cit.
49 *The Boonton Weekly Bulletin*, op. cit.
50 Ibid.
51 Ibid.

Charles Booth, the head, is a quiet and determined English Secularist who came to this country nearly forty years ago. His wife, Mrs. A. M. Booth, is one of those splendid women fit to be chief executive of a nation. The heroines who composed the choir are Miss Kate Booth, Miss Ada Booth, Miss Jessie Booth, and Miss Fannie Booth. The sons are Hubert, Charles and Thomas, manly young men, who would not be the first to seek a fight nor the first to leave one, when forced into it. With John Krahmer, a young Freethinker of New York, who was helping Mr. Reynolds in the work connected with the tent, they formed a guard that brought Mr. Reynolds out of the affair with whole bones and dry clothes. Before the advance of the Booth family, led by the intrepid mother, the crowd of roughs parted like sheep.[52]

The mob cut the main and auxiliary guy ropes and the center pole fell on the benches. They also slashed the canvas of the tent so that the tent was wrecked. It was estimated that the damage would cost several hundred dollars to repair.[53]

According to *The Boonton Weekly Bulletin*, Reynolds traveled to New York City on Thursday, July 29, 1886 to enroll the assistance of the famous attorney and freethinker Col. Robert G. Ingersoll, to defend him against the charge of blasphemy and to bring a claim against the Town of Boonton for failure to prevent damage to the lecture tent.[54] Later, speaking on the Boonton events before the Tenth Annual Congress of the

---

[52] "Reynolds Arrested for Blasphemy" *The Truth Seeker* Vol. 13, No. 32 August 7, 1886, p. 504.

[53] "On the Trial for Blasphemy: Col. Ingersoll's Defense of Charles B. Reynolds" *The New York Times* May 20, 1887, p. 8.

[54] *The New York Times*, Nov. 13, 1886, op. cit. Both Reynolds and Ingersoll were officers of the American Secular Union. Col. Robert G. Ingersoll was the President and Charles B. Reynolds was the Chairman of the Executive Committee. The subsequent grand jury indictment for blasphemy in Boonton, New Jersey was never brought to trial. Instead, a similar charge in Morristown, New Jersey was prosecuted. See "Jersey Law Triumphant: Reynolds Found Guilty of Blasphemy" *The New York Times*, May 21, 1887, p. 8.

American Secular Union at Chickering Hall in New York City on November 12, 1886, Reynolds had the following comments about his upcoming blasphemy trial:

It will come off in January [1887]. If Col. Ingersoll is well I think he may be able to persuade the jury to disagree. If he is ill I shall have to persuade my internal arrangements to agree with prison food. "In any case," said Mr. Reynolds, suddenly becoming dramatic, waving his arms, raising his voice, and stamping his feet, "if they kill me and if they kill my wife I have two sons who will avenge me. If they kill them I have a hundred friends who will avenge them." [Applause][55]

The common council of Boonton served Reynolds with an order prohibiting future lectures.

Boonton, N.J., July 30, 1886

MR. C. B. REYNOLDS, Sir: At a special meeting of the Common Council of the town of Boonton, held on Thursday evening, July 28, 1886, the following resolution was adopted: *Resolved,* That the town clerk be authorized to notify Mr. C. B. Reynolds that he is strictly forbidden to hold any more of his so-called Liberal but unlawful meetings within the corporate limits of the town of Boonton. In accordance with the above resolution you are hereby notified to discontinue all such meetings within the corporate limits.

By order of the Common Council of the town of Boonton.
JOHN DUNN, Town Clerk[56]

A hearing on the charge of blasphemy was held on Saturday, July 31, in the dining room of the U.S. Hotel in Boonton. The meeting location had been changed from the Station House because it was not large enough to accommodate the crowd that wished to be admitted. Justice of the Peace John A. Van Orden presided and

[55] *The New York Times*, Nov. 13, 1886, op. cit.

[56] "Reynolds Arrested for Blasphemy" The Truth Seeker Vol. 13, No. 32 August 7, 1886, p. 504.

Mr. N. S. Kitchel acted as counsel for the prosecution.[57] Reynolds represented himself in the proceedings but was assisted by E. M. MacDonald, editor of *The Truth Seeker*.[58] Reynolds was questioned prior to swearing an oath.

Reynolds upon being asked before taking the oath if he believed in God, replied that he and 'the old fellow,' referring to the deity, were not on intimate terms.[59]

The official record of the hearing was kept by Justice of the Peace Van Orden as follows:

STATE OF NEW JERSEY On Complaint of Wm Brown
VS. for Blasphemy
CHAS. B. REYNOLDS

Evidence of Wm. Brown.
Question by N. S. Kitchel, Esq.:
Did you attend a meeting held in a tent on the northerly side of Washington Street in Boonton?
Ans. By Wm. Brown:
I did.
Ques. by Mr. Kitchel:
Did you see this man Reynolds there?
Ans.: I did.
Ques.:
Tell us what he said.
Ans. By Brown:
Well he said that in a certain part of the Bible it said God made Everything the Birds the Beasts the Fishes & everything out of water and in another place it says that God made Adam out of dust
and he wanted to make a mate for Adam but the Old Man had used up all the Dust in making Adam so he did not know just what to do so he put Adam to sleep I don't know whether it was with Ether or Chloroform and took a rib out of Adam to make a Woman, now you all know if you took every Bone in a Man's Body it would not make

---

[57] *The Iron Era* Dover, N.J. August 7, 1886, p.1.
[58] "Reynolds Arrested for Blasphemy" The Truth Seeker Vol. 13, No. 32 August 7, 1886, p. 504.
[59] *The Iron Era* Dover, N.J. August 7, 1886, op. cit.

the Jaw of a Woman. Who believes any such nonsense. In that way he tried to ridicule the Bible & God and said he took a piece of a verse here & there.
Mr. Reynolds asked him if he knew of any verse that he took a part of?
Ans: No.
Cross-examined
Ques. by Mr. Reynolds:
Do you know that it was the Bible I was reading from?
Ans.:
I do not.
Ques.:
Are you familiar with the Bible? I guess not?
Brown did not answer.
Evidence of George Hessey.
Question by Mr. Kitchel:
Have you ever seen this man Reynolds or talked. Have you heard or had a conversation with him.
Question objected. Objection overruled.
Ans. By Hessey:
I have.
Mr. Kitchel:
Tell the Court what you know about him – Reynolds.
Ans. By Hessey:
I met Mr. Reynolds and Mr. Cramer. Mr. Reynolds asked me about what I thought of his Lectures
I answered him that I had a complete set of Ingersoll's works at home but I am satisfied that there is no truth in them nor in your Lectures.
(Objected to. Objection overruled.)
I believe the Bible is true, and your Lectures are nothing in them but ridicule. Mr. Reynolds' answer was that is our argument to ridicule and make fun.
The complainant then rested.
The defendant C. B. Reynolds then moved to dismiss the Complaint because it did not charge him the Defendant with Blasphemy, & said the words who believes such nonsense sworn to in the Complaint was stated there as the words of Brown the complainant and said if those words were Blasphemous Brown was the blasphemer. I refused to Dismiss the complaint as the words attributed to Brown by the Defendant were the words of the Defendant as I understood the complaint & as clearly appeared by the Testimony of Brown.
The Defendant then offered as evidence John Cramer.
Counsel for complainant objected to his being sworn because he was not competent he then Examined him on his Voire dire.
Question by Mr. Kitchel: Do you believe there is a God?

Answer: Yes.
Question: Do you believe the Bible is true?
Answer: No.
Question: What punishment will be administered to you if you swear Falsely?
Answer: I will be punished by the Laws of the state for perjury.
Question by Mr. Kitchel:
Do you believe any punishment will be inflicted upon you by almighty God if you swear Falsely?
Answer: I don't know.
Mr. Kitchel then read from Nixon's digest as follows unless the Witness believes there is a God who will punish him if he swears falsely he cannot be admitted as a witness.
I then asked the witness several questions concerning his respecting the Character and Attributes of God. He said he was an Agnostic & had no views on the subjects.
I then thought it clearly my duty to exclude him as a witness.
J. A. VAN ORDEN, J. P.[60]

In editorial remarks printed in *The Truth Seeker* on August 7, 1886, E. M. MacDonald gave a different version of events during the hearing. He pointed out that the complainant, Mr. Wm. Brown, was a self-described 'healer' for the Young Men's Christian Association and the Woman's Christian Temperance Union; that he admitted in his testimony that he was unfamiliar with the Bible verses that he says Reynolds ridiculed; and that George Hessey, the second witness against Reynolds, was not in fact present at the tent. Moreover, MacDonald said that the actual testimony by John Krahmer in reply to direct questions by Justice Van Order consisted of the following:

Justice Van Orden:
Q. What would God do to you if you tell a lie?
A. To the justice: What would he do to you?
Reply by the justice:
I don't know.

---

[60] "Reynolds Arrested for Blasphemy" *The Truth Seeker* Vol. 13, No. 32 August 7, 1886, pp. 504-505.

Answer by Mr. Krahmer to the first question:
Neither do I.
By the Court: Don't you know what you believe about future rewards and punishments?
A. No.
By the Court: Then you are not a competent witness.
By the Prosecution: The laws of New Jersey say you *must* believe something. New Jersey rules out Infidels, Freethinkers, and Truth Seekers.[61]

Justice Van Orden set bail at $400 and remanded the case to the grand jury of Morris County which was scheduled to meet at Morristown, N.J. on the second Tuesday of October 1886. Boonton city councilman James Maxfield paid the bail amount.[62]

The Truth Seeker editorial by E. M. MacDonald also recounted an interesting anecdote about Marshal Gilmartin who served the arrest warrant on Reynolds for the charge of blasphemy.

The marshal of Boonton is a Catholic named Gilmartin, and the priest of the parish told his father that if the marshal arrested any of the Catholics concerned in the attack upon the tent he, the priest, would turn the marshal out of the church. Afterward the priest publicly deprecated the destruction of the tent, but principally, we fear, upon the ground that the town would have to pay the damages.[63]

---

[61] "Reynolds Arrested for Blasphemy" *The Truth Seeker* Vol. 13, No. 32 August 7, 1886, p. 505. The use of the term "Truth Seekers" is clearly a reference to the presence of the editor of *The Truth Seeker* weekly.

[62] Ibid., p. 505. According to E. M. MacDonald, James Maxfield was, "one of the oldest and most respected residents of the town. His house, in the anti-slavery times, was one of the stations on the 'underground railway' which transported slaves to Canada, and he left the church because of its pro-slavery attitude."

[63] "Reynolds Arrested for Blasphemy" *The Truth Seeker* Vol. 13, No. 32 August 7, 1886, op. cit.

After the hearing, the townspeople called out many threats to Reynolds until he quit Boonton.

> 'Lynch him,' 'Tar and feather him,' 'Throw him in the canal,' and many more like expressions were heard on all sides. All that was lacking was someone to say 'go' and I doubt if the word had been given, that Reynolds or any of his clique would ever undertake the people of Boonton again that there was no God and that their religion was a farce.[64]

In the days following his arrest, Reynolds wrote a small pamphlet, *New Jersey and Her Laws*, which explained and challenged the state blasphemy law.

> When the fanatics of Boonton arrested him on July 28th, he [Reynolds] was indignant, and the most natural thing for him to do, it seemed, was to enlighten the people of that place as to what blasphemy laws are, and as to who are the real blasphemers. The first was done by circulating a pamphlet upon blasphemy, in which was pointed out the unconstitutionality, the barbarism, and the foolishness of such laws...[65]

The Truth Seeker published the pamphlet.[66] Reynolds returned to Boonton to distribute it.

> On Wednesday, the 11th inst. [Aug. 11, 1886], Mr. Reynolds invaded the place again [Boonton, N.J.], armed with hundreds of copies of a small pamphlet on blasphemy, being the *Truth Seeker* editorial of August 14th, with some additional paragraphs addressed specifically to the inhabitants of Morris County, New Jersey. These he distributed in all the stores, and in most of the houses. It is needless to say that the pamphlet was thoroughly read. The gossip and excitement resulting from the arrest had in a good measure subsided, but this second advent aroused the sleepy little town, and for the balance of the week blasphemy was again discussed. No violence was offered Mr. Reynolds, most of the rougher element being at work in the silk factory when the distribution was going on. The justice of

---

[64] *The Iron Era* Dover, N.J., August 7, 1886, p. 1.
[65] *The Truth Seeker* Vol. 13, No. 44, October 30, 1886, p. 696.
[66] "New Jersey and Her laws" *The Truth Seeker* Vol. 13, No. 33, August 14, 1886, p. 520.

the peace who held Mr. Reynolds to bail was encountered upon the street, and he extended his hand for a fraternal greeting. He got it, along with a pamphlet which had the needless effect of lengthening his Methodistical countenance about two inches.[67]

In his pamphlet, "New Jersey and Her Laws," Reynolds began by opposing the freedom of religion and freedom of speech guarantees contained in the New Jersey Constitution with the prohibition against blasphemy contained in statute.

The constitution and the statutes of New Jersey seem to conflict, and it is for the New Jersey courts to say which is valid. In article I of the Constitution adopted in 1844, the following is affirmed:
Sec. 4. No person shall be denied the enjoyment of any civil right merely on account of his religious principles.
Sec. 5. Every person may freely speak, write, and publish his sentiments on all subjects, being responsible for the abuse of that right. No law shall be passed to restrain or abridge the liberty of speech or of the press.
But among the crimes enumerated is one called blasphemy, which is borne upon by the following statute:
If any person shall willfully blaspheme the holy name of God, by denying, cursing, or contumeliously reproaching his being or providence, or by cursing or contumeliously reproaching Jesus Christ or the Holy Ghost, or the Christian religion or the holy word of God (that is, the canonical scriptures contained in the books of the Old and New Testaments), or by profane scoffing at or exposing them, or any of them, to contempt and ridicule, then every person so offending shall, on conviction thereof, be punished by a fine, not exceeding two hundred dollars, or imprisonment at hard labor not exceeding twelve months, or both.[68]

Reynolds continues, in "New Jersey and Her Laws," to identify a further conflict - between common law prohibitions against testimony by irreligious persons and

---

[67] "Boonton Again Awakened" *The Truth Seeker* Vol. 13, No. 34, August 21, 1886, p. 536.

[68] "New Jersey and Her Laws" *The Truth Seeker* Vol. 13, No. 33, August 14, 1886, p. 520. "Contumeliously" means in a manner intended to convey contempt.

statute law allowances for witnesses to make an affirmation in lieu of swearing an oath.

The common law of the state in regard to witnesses, as formulated by Nixon's Digest (from 1709 to 1868, 4th ed.) is this:
Persons not of the Christian religion may be sworn according to the ceremonies of their religion, as a Mohammedan on the Koran, etc. But unless the person believes there is a God who will punish him if he swears falsely, he cannot be admitted as a witness.
...The Revised Statutes of New Jersey, published in 1877, containing the following:
26. That every person who shall be permitted or required to take an oath in any case where by law an oath is allowed or required, and who shall allege that he or she is conscientiously scrupulous of taking an oath, shall, instead of the form of an oath, be permitted to make his or her solemn affirmation or declaration; and if such person shall choose to affirm, it shall be in words following, to wit: "I, ________, do solemnly, sincerely, and truly declare and affirm."[69]

Reynolds concluded by comparing the wording in the blasphemy law in New Jersey and the blasphemy law in Massachusetts that was used to convict and imprison Abner Kneeland more than fifty years previously.

In 1834, when Abner Kneeland was imprisoned for saying, "Universalists believe in a god which I do not; but believe that their god, with his moral attributes (aside from nature itself), is nothing but a chimera of their own imagination"...[70]

Later, on October 8, 1886, Reynolds visited Boonton again and distributed a second pamphlet, "Blasphemy and the Bible." That pamphlet was published with an illustration, "Casting pearls before swine," and priced for sale at 10 cents. The contents of the second pamphlet were published in *The Truth Seeker* in two

---

[69] Ibid., p. 520.
[70] Ibid., p. 520.

parts in the issues of Saturday, October 9, 1886 and Saturday, October 16, 1886.[71]

I return to New York city on Monday. *The Truth Seeker* company are getting out my pamphlet, "Blasphemy and the Bible," to be ready on my arrival in New York so I can at once visit Boonton and Morristown and personally distribute about fifteen hundred copies among the people.[72]

In his pamphlet, "Blasphemy and the Bible," Reynolds prepared a reply to the charge that his lectures in Boonton blasphemed God. To make his defense, Reynolds chose to quote verses from the Bible to demonstrate that it blasphemed God. He believed that merely repeating Holy Scripture could not constitute blasphemy.

…pamphlet showing that Christians and their Bible were the real blasphemers, inasmuch as they ascribe to God sentiments, passions, and attributes which degrade him to the level of a Nero – an inhuman and bloodthirsty monster. This pamphlet called "Blasphemy and the Bible," shows that the Bible is God's worst enemy, and that, in circulating the book, Christians are destroying his good character.[73]

---

[71] Vol. 13, No. 41, pp. 646-647 and Vol. 13, No. 42, pp. 658-659.

[72] *The Truth Seeker* Vol. 13, No. 41, October 9, 1886, p. 645.

[73] *The Truth Seeker* Vol. 13, No. 44, October 30, 1886, p. 696. See also, David Lawton *Blasphemy* London: Harvester Wheatsheaf (1993), p. 134:

The pamphlet accuses the Bible of giving 'blasphemous representations of God': 'Is it possible to concede more horrible blasphemy than this holy Bible contains?' It urges that the best things in the Bible come from the wisdom Moses gained from the Egyptians (Acts 7:22): Reynolds too was most likely a freemason. 'The Bible is simply a barbarous history of a barbarous people' (p. 5), with a 'silly story' for an account of Creation (p. 7), and a parodic rendering of the Bible's teaching, especially on the incarnation and life of Jesus…

Reynolds began this pamphlet by questioning the origins and truth of the Bible. He referred to Babylonian and Egyptian creation myths that were extant long before the Jewish stories.

All of the ideas given of the creation and fall of man are of pagan origin. The Egyptian god, Neff, the creator, formed man's body of clay on a potter's wheel. The Babylonians had the legend of the creation and fall of man fifteen hundred years before the Hebrews heard of it.[74]

Reynolds pointed out that the Bible contains conflicting narratives of creation in Genesis and he cites the controversial book of Bishop John W. Colenso which explicates it.

...Dean Stanley says: 'It is clear to the diligent student of the Bible that the first and second chapters of Genesis contain two narratives of the creation side by side, differing from each other in almost every particular of time, place, and order.' Bishop Colenso, in his great work, The Pentateuch Examined, vol. ii, pp. 171-3, calls attention to the most noticeable contradictions in the two cosmogonies." [75]

---

[74] "Blasphemy and the Bible" *The Truth Seeker* Part I of II, Vol. 13, No. 41, October 9, 1886, p. 646

[75] Ibid, p. 646. Bishop Colenso summarized contradictions that he found in the biblical story of Creation contained in Genesis. These contradictions had long been known and were the subject of considerable debate by biblical scholars. According to Colenso, the first account of Creation was at Genesis i.1-ii.3 and was written by an unknown author who always referred to God as Elohim. The second account, Colenso said, was at Genesis ii.4-25 and was written by a different author who referred to God as Jehovah. One example of differences in the two cosmogonies was that, in the first account, the birds and beasts were created before man (Gen. i.20,24,26) while, in the second account, man was created before the birds and beasts (Gen. ii.7, 19). Colenso commented on contradictions regarding the biblical story of the Deluge. For instance, one account states that two of every living thing, male and female, were brought into the Ark (Gen. vi.19-20), while, another account states that seven of "clean" beasts and two of unclean beasts were led into the Ark (Gen. vii.2-3). See Rev. John William Colenso D.D. *The Pentateuch and Book of*

In order to advance his argument, Reynolds used strong ridicule when relating passages from the Bible. The grand jury found that this ridicule supported a charge of blasphemy under state law. For example, Reynolds wrote the following when describing the creation story in Genesis.

Gen. i, 12, declares the fowls came forth from the waters. Gen. ii, 19, declares the fowls came forth from the ground. Gen. i, 27 declares man and woman were created together. Gen. ii, 10, declares that man, birds, beasts and creeping things were all created before woman. Woman was an afterthought. God at first thought Adam could propagate alone; but after he made all other animals in pairs – male and female – he discovered his mistake, but seems to have nothing left to make woman of, so he put Adam to sleep, stole one of his ribs, and made a woman of it (Gen. ii, 21, 22). And if you don't believe this silly story you are an Infidel, and under Jersey law must be sent to prison for a year and fined two hundred dollars.[76]

The "Fall of Man" provided Reynolds with another target of ridicule as well as an argument against the Bible as a moral guide.

We read in the Bible that God placed Adam and Eve in the garden of Eden, constituted them so they could not resist temptation, then

---

Joshua Critically Examined Part II New York: D. Appleton and Company (1864), pp. 54-58.
According to Archbishop Ussher, Adam was created on the sixth day – October 28, 4004 BC (Friday). Subsequently, Adam was turned out of Paradise on the tenth day of the world or November 1, 4004 BC. Adam lived 930 years and died 3,074 years before Christ. Noah was born in 2948 BC, the tenth generation from Adam. The Deluge started on December 7, 2349 BC (Sunday). Noah died in 1998 BC, 350 years after the Deluge and he lived 950 years. See James Ussher [Archbishop of Armagh and Primate of All Ireland]. *The Annals of the World: Deduced from the Origin of Time, and continued to the beginning of the Emperour Vespasian's Reign, and the total Destruction and Abolition of the Temple and Common-wealth of the Jews. Containing the History of the Old and New Testament, with that of the Macchabees.* London. Printed by E. Tyler (MDCLVIII).
[76] Ibid, p. 646.

placed temptation continually before them, knowing they must fall; to make assurance doubly sure he creates a subtle devil to beguile them, insuring their fall; then damns them for falling, and damns all the human race...[77]

Finally, Reynolds summarized the differences between Secularists and Christians in the conclusion to his pamphlet.

If Truth is not loved for her own pure sake; if to lead a noble life; if to make men happier; if to spread brightness around us; if to leave the world better than we found it – if these aims have no attraction for us, if these thoughts cannot inspire us, then we are not worthy to be Secularists, we have no right to the proud title of truth seekers. If you want to be paid for your good lives by living forever in a lazy, useless fashion in an idle heaven; if you want to be bribed into nobility of life; if, like silly children, you learn your lesson, not to gain knowledge, but to win sugar-plums, then you had better cling to your creeds and your churches. They are good enough for you; you are not worthy to be free.[78]

In the pamphlet, "Blasphemy and the Bible," Reynolds attempted to put the Bible and Christianity on trial instead of himself. He believed that a charge of

---

[77] "Blasphemy and the Bible – Continued" *The Truth Seeker* Part II of II, Vol. 13, No. 42, October 16, 1886, p. 658.
The Victorian poet Edward FitzGerald immortalized this injustice in his celebrated poem, "The Rubaiyat of Omar Khayyam," published anonymously in 1859. Verses LVII and LVIII:

> Oh, Thou, who didst with Pitfall and with Gin
> Beset the Road I was to wander in,
> Thou wilt not with Predestination round
> Enmesh me, and impute my Fall to Sin?
>
> Oh, Thou, who Man of baser Earth didst make,
> And who with Eden didst devise the Snake;
> For all the Sin wherewith the Face of Man
> Is blacken'd, Man's Forgiveness give – and take!

[78] Ibid., p. 658.

blasphemy was absurd given the content of the Bible and the history of the Christian church.

During early October 1886, Reynolds visited Mr. Willard W. Cutler at the district attorney's office in Morristown, New Jersey, about 30 miles from New York City.

On my return to New York City after the convention of the New York Freethinkers' Association at White Sulphur Springs, I visited the district-attorney at Morristown, N.J. He informed me that the grand jury would sit on the second Tuesday in October, and most likely be discharged on the Friday or Saturday following, and that my trial would not take place till two weeks from date of the discharge of the grand jury. I had the privilege to look over the district-attorney's law library, and found the law very clear and positive on the crime of blasphemy. There is little possibility of my escaping indictment. Col. R. G. Ingersoll, who, with his characteristic chivalrous generosity and devotion to the cause of liberty, has pledged himself to defend me, expresses confidence that my trial at Morristown will be before an intelligent jury and that the case will be laughed out of court. In any other state than New Jersey or Delaware beyond a doubt this would be so. But New Jersey bigots and fanatics are not apt to be jovial, nor to possess sufficient intelligence to appreciate a joke. New Jersey Christians, of whom the jury will be composed, are predisposed by nature and long habit to make egregious asses of themselves, and to act the merciless fanatic with grim, owl-like solemnity – all for the glory of Jesus. But my dependence is in the great ability of my counsel and the intelligence of the Supreme Court as beyond all question the statute law is contrary to the Constitution of New Jersey, as well as the Constitution of the United States.[79]

---

[79] "The Blasphemer's Program" *The Truth Seeker* Vol. 13, No. 41, October 9, 1886, pp. 644-645. Reynolds' own account of the blasphemy charges pending before the grand jury appears to indicate that he expected to be convicted at the trial court level but that the constitutionality of the blasphemy statute would ultimately be settled by the New Jersey Supreme Court or possibly the U.S. Supreme Court. There is no evidence, however, that the blasphemy law violation was deliberate to provoke a test case for appeal. Quite the contrary, Reynolds' unfamiliarity with the law seems to be proof that

There were two legal issues raised by the Boonton blasphemy case. Reynolds correctly anticipated them in his pamphlet, "New Jersey and Her Laws." First, the New Jersey constitution, adopted in 1844, states at Article I, Section 5, that:

> Every person may freely speak, write, and publish his sentiments on all subjects, being responsible for the abuse of that right. No law shall be passed to restrain or abridge the liberty of speech or of the press.[80]

However, the statute laws of New Jersey, effective in 1886, state that *ridiculing* God, the Bible, or the Christian religion constituted the crime of blasphemy:

> If any person shall willfully blaspheme the holy name of God, by denying, cursing, or contumeliously reproaching His being or providence, or by cursing or contumeliously reproaching Jesus Christ or the Holy Ghost, or the Christian religion or the holy word of God (that is the canonical scriptures contained in the books of the Old and New Testaments), or by profane scoffing at or exposing them, or any of them, to contempt and ridicule, then every person so offending shall, on conviction thereof, be punished by a fine, not exceeding two hundred dollars, or imprisonment at hard labor, not exceeding twelve months, or both.[81]

Second, New Jersey common law with respect to witnesses, as stated in *Nixon's Digest 1709-1868* (4th ed.) requires,

> Persons not of the Christian religion may be sworn according to the ceremonies of their religion, as a Mohammedan on the Koran, etc.

---

the blasphemy charge was unanticipated. And, his conviction was not appealed.

[80] New Jersey Constitution (1844) published by F. S. Mills & C. Brittain.

[81] *Revision of the Statutes of New Jersey: Published Under the Authority of the Legislature by Virtue of an Act Approved April 4, 1871* Trenton, N.J.: John L. Murphy, Book and Job Printer (1877), p. 238.

But unless the person believes there is a God who will punish him if he swears falsely, he cannot be admitted as a witness.[82]

However, the Revised Statutes of New Jersey (1877), state that a witness may make an affirmation instead of swearing an oath thereby rendering belief in a deity irrelevant.

26.That every person who shall be permitted or required to take an oath in any case where by law an oath is allowed or required, and who shall allege that he or she is conscientiously scrupulous of taking an oath, shall, instead of the form of an oath, be permitted to make his or her solemn affirmation or declaration; and if such person shall choose to affirm, it shall be in words following, to wit: 'I _____, do solemnly, sincerely, and truly declare and affirm.'[83]

Reynolds expected that the trial court or appellate court would resolve the conflicts between statute law and common law with the state and federal constitutions.

---

[82] *Nixon's Digest 1709-1868*, 4th ed. Published by Martin R. Dennis & Co., p. 1055. Attorney Colonel Robert G. Ingersoll, who defended Reynolds in his blasphemy trial, had only contempt for the practice of having witnesses swear oaths. In a letter, dated March 31, 1882, to George Jacob Holyoake, a famous freethinker in England who coined the term "secularism," Ingersoll wrote the following:
I regard the entire oath business as perfectly absurd. It has no effect on honest men, and can be taken advantage of by rogues. Most jurors place all testimony on an equality, because the witnesses have been sworn. The oath is the best friend that falsehood has. It is the solemn mask of a lie. I would like to see all oaths abolished. The good and bad should not be put on a level in a court of justice.
Eva Ingersoll Wakefield. *The Letters of Robert G. Ingersoll* Westport, CT: Greenwood Press, Publishers (1973) [reprint of original 1951 edition from the Philosophical Library, New York], p. 255.

[83] *Revision of the Statutes of New Jersey: Published Under the Authority of the Legislature by Virtue of an Act Approved April 4, 1871* Trenton, N.J.: John L. Murphy, Book and Job Printer (1877), p. 904.

Abner Kneeland, formerly a Unitarian preacher, was convicted and jailed for violating a similar blasphemy statute in Massachusetts in 1835 for stating that he disbelieved in God.[84] One of the counts of blasphemy was based upon letters to the editor of the Universalist *Trumpet*, a religious periodical, where he wrote:

1. Universalists believe in a god which I do not; but believe that their god with all his moral attributes (aside from nature itself) is nothing more than a chimera of their own imagination.
2. Universalists believe in Christ, which I do not; but believe that the whole story concerning him is as much a fable and fiction as that of the god Prometheus, the tragedy of whose death is said to have been acted on the stage in the theatre at Athens, 500 years before the Christian era.
3. Universalists believe in miracles, which I do not; but believe that every pretension to them can either be accounted for on natural principles or else is to be attributed to mere trick and imposture.
4. Universalists believe in the resurrection of the dead, immortality and eternal life, which I do not; but believe that all life is mortal, that

---

84 "New Jersey and Her Laws" *The Truth Seeker* Vol. 13, No. 33 August 14, 1886, p. 520.
Abner Kneeland wrote about his trials in two volumes: Abner Kneeland. *An Introduction to the Defence of Abner Kneeland, Charged with Blasphemy; before the Municipal Court, in Boston, Mass. at the January Term, in 1834* Boston: Printed for the Publisher (1834) and Abner Kneeland. *A Review of the Trial, Conviction, and Final Imprisonment in the Common Jail of the County of Suffolk, of Abner Kneeland, for the Alleged Crime of Blasphemy* Boston: George A. Chapman (1838).
Other accounts of the trials were published contemporaneously: *Report of the Arguments of the Attorney of the Commonwealth, at the Trials of Abner Kneeland, for Blasphemy, in the Municipal and Supreme Courts, in Boston, January and May, 1834* Boston: Beals, Homer & Co. (1834) and *Speech of Abner Kneeland, Delivered before the Supreme Court of the City of Boston, in his Own Defence, on an Indictment for Blasphemy November Term 1834* Boston: J. Q. Adams (1834).

death is an eternal extinction of life to the individual who possesses it, and that no individual life is, ever was, or ever will be eternal.[85]

The Massachusetts act against blasphemy was enacted in 1782 and the language was largely copied into the later New Jersey blasphemy statute. The Massachusetts act stated, in part, that:

Be it enacted by the Senate and House of Representatives in General Court assembled, and by authority of the same, That if any person shall willfully blaspheme the holy name of God, by denying, cursing, or contumeliously reproaching God, his creation, government, or final judging of the world, or by cursing, reproaching Jesus Christ, or the Holy Ghost, or by cursing, or contumeliously reproaching the Holy Word of God, that is, the canonical scriptures, contained in the books of the Old and New Testaments, or exposing them, or any part of them, to contempt and ridicule…every person so offending shall be punished by imprisonment not exceeding twelve months, by sitting in the pillory, by whipping, or by sitting on the

---

[85] Leonard W. Levy (ed.). *Blasphemy in Massachusetts: Freedom of Conscience and the Abner Kneeland Case, A Documentary Record* New York: Da Capo Press (1973), p.37. In other writings, Kneeland was more explicit about his atheism. For example, in the appendix to the third edition of a book containing lectures he made in New York City, Kneeland challenged the clergy about the evidences of Christianity as follows:
The truth of all their dogmas which relate to God, to heaven, to hell, and to a future state of existence for man, in their sense of speaking, is called in question. The whole is treated as an idle chimera. Out of the multiplicity of opinions, taught for solemn truth, in relation to supernatural operations, as well as to unseen beings and an unknown world, beyond the present life, after eighteen hundred years' preaching, the clergy are unable to prove anything true for man beyond the grave. They are unable to prove the existence of what is called God, on which all other theological opinions depend. Hence the presumption is, that all those opinions are false.
See, Abner Kneeland. *A Review of the Evidences of Christianity; in a Series of Lectures, Delivered in Broadway Hall, New-York, August, 1829* 6th ed., Boston: Office of the Investigator (1835), p. 193. [orig. published in 1829].

gallows, with a rope about the neck, or binding to the good behavior, at the discretion of the Supreme Judicial Court before whom the conviction may be, according to the aggravation of the offence.[86]

The State of Massachusetts prosecuted Abner Kneeland under both the statute and common law.[87] The defense pursued two arguments: "the case is not within the statute, on which the indictment is founded, and that the Statute is in violation of the letter and spirit of the Constitution."[88] About 50 years later, Charles Reynolds faced similar charges and made a similar defense. Kneeland's comments on his conviction and jail sentence were clearly shared by Reynolds.

So long as Christianity will make use of civil power…for its support, or to aid in its propagation, so long will it carry demonstration to every rational and reflecting mind that it is not based on divine truth, that it is all craft, that it was got up by man for the aggrandizement of a few, and to support them in idleness and luxury at the expense of the ignorance, credulity and hard earnings of the many. If Christians, therefore, believe what they pretend and profess to believe, let them put their faith on a level with unbelief; let them meet unbelievers on fair and open ground…[89]

---

[86] Leonard W. Levy (ed.). *Blasphemy in Massachusetts: Freedom of Conscience and the Abner Kneeland Case, A Documentary Record* New York: Da Capo Press (1973), p.46.

[87] [Samuel D. Parker]. *Report of the Arguments of the Attorney of the Commonwealth at the Trials of Abner Kneeland, for Blasphemy, in the Municipal and Supreme Court, in Boston, January and May, 1834* (Collected and published at the request of some Christians of various denominations) Boston: Printed by Beals, Homer & Co. (1834), p. 4.

[88] Leonard W. Levy (ed.). *Blasphemy in Massachusetts: Freedom of Conscience and the Abner Kneeland Case, A Documentary Record* op. cit., p. 50.

[89] Ibid., p. 510. From a letter written by Abner Kneeland on June 19, 1838 while he served a 60-day sentence in the Boston jail for a blasphemy conviction. Originally published in: Abner Kneeland. *A Review of the Trial, Conviction, and Final Imprisonment in the Common Jail of the County of Suffolk, of Abner Kneeland, for the*

Grand Jury Indictment

After Reynolds left Boonton, New Jersey, not much is known about his activities. He continued lecturing. As already noted, he visited Morristown, New Jersey during early October in order to speak with the district attorney to learn about the upcoming grand jury proceedings and review the blasphemy statute. While there, he distributed copies of his article, "Blasphemy and the Bible." The article, "Blasphemy and the Bible," had been published in *The Truth Seeker*.[90]

I did all in my power while at Morristown to help the people there to an appreciation of truth and the need of investigation. I circulated twenty-five copies of *The Truth Seeker* with the "Pearls Before Swine" cartoon, which were eagerly received.[91]

The pamphlet included an illustration of Reynolds lecturing in Boonton, New Jersey prior to his arrest on blasphemy charges – the "Pearls Before Swine" cartoon.[92]

...[Reynolds] had inserted a two-page cut to illustrate his idea of Boonton. At the back was the tent. His own figure was the central one in front. He carried a basket from which he was scattering pearls before a lot of swine, some marked with a cross and others with an 'M'. The swine appeared to be coming from pens marked, "M. E. Hog Pen" and "Pig Sty of the Holy Virgin," and the pens were

---

Alleged Crime of Blasphemy Boston: George A. Chapman (1838), p. 50.

90 "To Be Tried for Blasphemy", *The New York Times*, October 28, 1886, p.8.

91 "The Blasphemer's Program" *The Truth Seeker* Vol. 13, No. 41, October 9, 1886, p. 645.

92 "The Morristown pamphlet, a slight variation of the one Reynolds circulated in Boonton, was particularly obnoxious to the Methodists and Catholics because of a cartoon, based on the Boonton uproar, which adorned the front cover." Orvin Larson. *American Infidel: Robert G. Ingersoll* New York: The Citadel Press (1962), p. 215.

guarded by a priest whose bucket was labeled "Catholic swill" and by a dominic with "Methodist slop" pained on a bucket he carried. Both of these figures carried bludgeons, with which they menaced the hog feeder. Over the priest's head was a guideboard naming Boonton as the spot near which the scene was supposed to take place.[93]

On October 13, 1886, Reynolds returned to Morristown, New Jersey for the Grand Jury proceedings. Again, he distributed copies of his pamphlet, "Blasphemy and the Bible."

Mr. Reynolds appeared in Morristown with this pamphlet on Oct. 13. A Boonton delegation was there clamoring for his indictment for blasphemy. He went to the hall outside the Grand Jury room, and while waiting there to hear what the Grand Jury were going to do with him, gave a few of the pamphlets to the doorkeeper and to others. Then he walked through the business part of the city and left pamphlets in some of the stores. Winfield West, the city bill poster, met him and asked if he had a license. He said he had not, and tried to arrange with West to distribute the pamphlets for him.[94]

---

93 "On Trial for Blasphemy", *The New York Times*, May 20, 1887, p.8.

94 Ibid., p. 8. The grand jury indictment issued on October 19, 1886 charged Reynolds with blasphemy on October 8, 1886 in Boonton, New Jersey. A second indictment would be issued in May 1887 and charge Reynolds with blasphemy on October 13, 1886 in Morristown, New Jersey.
Madalyn O'Hair incorrectly stated that, "An indictment was had on October 19, 1886 with Reynolds charged with one blasphemy at Boonton and a second at Morristown." Her article, "Trial of C. B. Reynolds for Blasphemy," appeared in *The American Atheist* issues for October, November and December 1986 in celebration of the centennial of the blasphemy arrest at Boonton, New Jersey. O'Hair may have relied upon erroneous information in published sources. For example, Orvin Larson. *American Infidel: Robert G. Ingersoll* New York: The Citadel Press (1962), p. 214, stated: "On October 13, Reynolds appeared in Morristown, New Jersey, not to hold meetings but to distribute pamphlets. A Boonton delegation, hearing he was there, arrived on the scene and demanded his indictment for blasphemy. A grand jury, then in session, found under a statute from early colonial days two indictments against him, blasphemy in Boonton and blasphemy at Morristown."

The Morris County Grand Jury returned an indictment on October 19, 1886 with two charges of blasphemy specifying that Reynolds circulated his pamphlet, "Blasphemy and the Bible" in Boonton on October 8, 1886. The indictment was founded on the evidence provided solely by the pamphlet and not the lectures he gave in Boonton which led to his arrest.

The indictment consisted of a summary of the blasphemy law and cited numerous statements from the pamphlet to illustrate the charges that were referred to trial.

MORRIS OYER AND TERMINER
AND GENERAL JAIL DELIVERY

OCT TERM, A.D. 1886

MORRIS COUNTY TO WIT:

The Grand Jury inquest for the State of New Jersey in and for the body of the county of Morris upon their oath present that Charles B. Reynolds late of the township of Boonton in the county of Morris aforesaid on the eighth day of October, 1886 at the township of Boonton aforesaid in the county of Morris aforesaid and within the jurisdiction of this court, unlawfully and wickedly did willfully blaspheme the Holy name of God by contumeliously reproaching his Being and Providence and by contumeliously reproaching Jesus Christ, and the Holy Word of God, that is, the canonical scriptures contained in the Old and New Testaments, and by profane scoffing at and exposing them to contempt and ridicule in that he, the said Charles B. Reynolds, did then and there publish, circulate and distribute a certain scandalous impious and blasphemous printed document entitled "Blasphemy and the Bible" by Charles B. Reynolds in which there were and are contained among other things certain scandalous, impious, and blasphemous matters and things to the tenor and effect following;

"This Bible describes God as so loving that He drowned the whole world in His mad fury, because it was so much worse than He (knowing all things) ever supposed it could be. An All-wise, unchangeable God, who got out of patience with a world which was just what His own stupid blundering had made it, and knew no better way out of the muddle than to destroy it by drowning!"

And in another part of the aforesaid printed document there were and was contained, among other things, certain other scandalous, impious, and blasphemous matter and things of the purport and effect following, to wit: "The Bible God says His people made Him jealous, provoked Him to anger, and now He will raise the mischief with them; for He declares His anger burns like Hell. He will destroy them all "Were it not that I feared the wrath of the enemy"- The Almighty God afraid of His enemies! Can the human mind conceive of more horrid blasphemy? Can even a New Jersey Christian believe such stuff was ever inspired by a God?

WHAT THE BIBLE REALLY TEACHES.

The Old Testament records for our instruction in morals the most foul and bestial instances of fornication, incest, and polygamy, perpetrated by God's own pet Saints and the New Testament indorses [sic] these lecherous old wretches as examples for all good Christians to follow."

And in another part of the aforesaid printed document there were and are contained among other things certain other scandalous, impious and blasphemous matter and things of the purport and effect following, that is to say:

"Now, reader, take time and calmly think it over. A Jewish girl becomes the mother of God Almighty – the mother of your God. The child of this young Jewess was God. Christ is God. God cried and screamed, squealed and kicked; God flung about His little arms; God made aimless dashes into space with his little fists; God stared foolishly at His own little toes; God smiled when He was comfortable and howled when pricked by an nasty pin; God was nursed at Mary's breast; God was wrapped in little diapers; God lay in a cradle and was rocked to sleep; God was quite sick when cutting His little teeth; God caught the measles, mumps, whooping cough, and scarlet fever; God learned to walk and often tumbled down bumped his forehead and made His little nose bleed; God was spanked when He was naughty, etc, etc."

Contrary to the form of the statute in such case made and provided and against the peace of this state the government and dignity of the same.

And the grand inquest aforesaid, upon their oath aforesaid, do further present that Charles B. Reynolds, late of the township of Boonton in the county of Morris aforesaid on the eighth day of October, 1886, at the township of Boonton aforesaid and within the jurisdiction of this court, with force and arms disregarding the laws of this state and profanely deriding and intending to bring the Holy Scriptures and the Christian religion into disbelief and contempt among the people of this state, unlawfully and wickedly did compose, print, and publish and did cause and procure to be composed, printed, and published a certain scandalous, impious, and blasphemous libel of and concerning God, and of and concerning the Holy Scriptures, and of and concerning the Christian religion, which libel is published and contained in a certain printed document entitled "Blasphemy and the Bible," by Charles B. Reynolds, in which said libel so printed published and composed, and so caused and procured to be composed, printed, and published as aforesaid by the said Charles B. Reynolds, the said Charles B. Reynolds did willfully blaspheme the Holy Name of God by denying and contumeliously reproaching His Being and Providence and by contumeliously reproaching Jesus Christ and the Christian religion and the Holy Name of God.

In one part of which scandalous and blasphemous libel, among other things, there were and are contained certain scandalous, impious, and blasphemous matter, and things of and concerning God and of and concerning His Providence, according to the purport and effect following to wit;

"The Bible describes God as so loving that He drowned the whole world in His mad fury, because it was so much worse than He (knowing all things!) ever supposed it could be. An all-wise, unchangeable God, who got out of patience with a world which was just what His own stupid blundering had made it, and He knew no better way out of the muddle than to destroy it by drowning!"

And in another part of said libel there were and are contained certain scandalous, impious, and blasphemous matter and things of and concerning God of and concerning His Being, and of and concerning the Holy Scriptures, and of an concerning the Christian religion according to the purport and effect following to wit:

"The Bible God says His people made Him jealous, provoked Him to anger, and now He will raise the mischief with them, for He declares His anger burns like Hell. He will destroy then all "Were it not that I feared the wrath of the enemy"

"The Almighty God afraid of His enemies! Can the human mind conceive of more horrid blasphemy? Can even a New Jersey Christian believe such stuff was ever inspired by a God?"
WHAT THE BIBLE REALLY TEACHES.

The Old Testament records for our instruction in morals the most foul and bestial instances of fornication, incest, and polygamy perpetrated by God's own pet Saints and the New Testament indorses [sic] these lecherous old wretches as examples for all good Christians to follow"

And in another part of said libel there were and are contained scandalous, impious, and blasphemous matters and things of and concerning God and of and concerning His Being and of and concerning Holy Scriptures and of and concerning the Christian religion and to the purport and effect following to wit:

Now, reader, take time and calmly think it over. A Jewish girl becomes the mother of God Almighty – the mother of your God; the child of this young Jewess was God; Christ is God; God cried and screamed, squealed and kicked; God flung about His little arms; God made aimless dashes into space with His little fists; God stared foolishly at His own little toes; God smiled when He was comfortable and howled when pricked by a nasty pin; God was nursed at Mary's breast; God was wrapped in little diapers; God lay in a cradle and was rocked to sleep; God was quite sick when cutting His little teeth; God caught the measles, mumps, whooping cough, and scarlet fever; God learned to walk and often tumbled down, bumped His forehead and made His little nose bleed; God was spanked when He was naughty, etc. etc.

To the great scandal and contumelious reproach of God, His Being and Providence and of Jesus Christ and the Christian religion and the Holy Word of God, contrary to the form of the statute in such case made and provided and against the peace of this state, the government and dignity of the same.

(signed) Willard W. Cutler
Prosecutor of Morris County[95]

It is possible that the cartoon in the pamphlet, "Casting pearls before swine," may have been responsible, in part, for curiously redundant charges of blasphemy in the indictment since the cartoon ridiculed the Christian religion and, specifically, the Methodist and Catholic churches in Boonton, New Jersey. However, Reynolds himself didn't believe this to be the case.

The pamphlet, "Blasphemy and the Bible," was simply a defense of my views and principles. The cartoon may or may not be in bad taste. I call attention to the fact that it was not referred to in the indictment under which I was tried.[96]

---

[95] The indictment was printed in *The Truth Seeker*, Vol. 13, No. 44, October 30, 1886, p. 696. It also appeared in *The Truth Seeker Annual and Freethinkers' Almanac 1887*, pp. 22-24.

[96] "A Letter from Mr. Reynolds" *The Truth Seeker* Vol. 14, No. 23, June 4, 1887, p. 357.

The second charge of blasphemy introduced the term "blasphemous libel" and found that, Reynolds' speech in his pamphlet was, "...profanely deriding and intending to bring the Holy Scriptures and the Christian religion into disbelief and contempt among the people of this state..."[97]

Later, Judge Childs would elaborate on the meaning of "blasphemous libel" in his instructions to the jury at the conclusion of the Reynolds blasphemy trial.

> You will notice that the defendant is on trial for libel, and it is called a blasphemous libel, because it denies and contumeliously reproaches the holy name of God; because it contumeliously reproaches Jesus Christ and the holy word of God. Blasphemy consists in the denial of the being, attributes, or nature of, or uttering impious and profane things against, God or the authority of the holy scriptures; but it is only committed by uttering such things in a scoffing and railing manner, out of a reproachful disposition, as it were, in the speaker, rather than with any purpose of propagating his irreverent opinion.
>
> If he has merely asserted his disbelief in all the popular notions of Christianity, without attempting by impious and abusive or blasphemous remarks to wound the feelings of the whole Christian community, he will not have committed an offense of which the law can take notice.[98]

On Monday, October 25, 1886, Reynolds was required to report to Morristown to submit his plea to the indictment. He advised the court that his counsel was unable to appear on the date set for trial just two days later. Attorney Col. Robert Ingersoll had agreed to represent Reynolds but was under instructions from his physician not to speak above a whisper following a recent surgery to remove an obstruction from his throat.

---

[97] The indictment was printed in *The Truth Seeker*, Vol. 13, No. 44, October 30, 1886, p. 696.

[98] "Convicted and Fined" *The Truth Seeker*, Vol. 14, No. 22, May 28, 1887, pp. 344-345.

Initially, Judge Francis Child refused to move the trial date and ordered Reynolds to find other counsel. Reynolds tried, without success, to engage other leading attorneys, including district attorney Charles Winfield and Judge Garrison of Jersey City.

Col. Ingersoll was present in court on Wednesday, October 27, 1886 and made a motion to set the case over to the next term for trial. Judge Child agreed and adjourned the case until Tuesday, January 18, 1887.[99] The original bail provided by Edwin Worman was renewed. Subsequently, the trial was moved to Tuesday, February 1, 1887 then Friday, May 20, 1887.[100]

Reynolds reported to the courthouse in Morristown, New Jersey on May 3, 1887 to learn the disposition of his blasphemy case. He was accompanied by Edwin Worman of Boonton, his bondsman; John Maxfield of Boonton; E.M. MacDonald, editor of *The Truth Seeker*; and L.K. Washburn, another freethought lecturer. District-attorney Williard W. Cutler and the presiding judge set the case for trial on Monday, May 16, 1887.[101]

A grand jury was convened on May 3, 1887 and it issued a second indictment for blasphemy on October 13, 1886 in Morristown, New Jersey.

MORRIS OYER AND TERMINER
AND GENERAL JAIL DELIVERY

MAY TERM, A.D. 1887

---

[99] "Blasphemy: Reynolds Indicted for the Crime of Libeling a Ghost" *The Truth Seeker* Vol. 13, No. 44, October 30, 1886, pp. 696-697.

[100] *The Truth Seeker* Vol. 14, No. 2, January 8, 1887, p. 25 and *The Truth Seeker* Vol. 14, No. 6, February 5, 1887, p. 5.

[101] "The Weary Way of the Blasphemer" *The Truth Seeker* Vol. 14, No. 20, May 14, 1887, p. 312.

MORRIS COUNTY TO WIT:

The Grand Jury inquest for the State of New Jersey in and for the body of the county of Morris upon their oath present that Charles B. Reynolds late of the township of Morris in the county of Morris aforesaid on the thirteenth day of October in the year of our Lord one thousand eight hundred and eighty six at the township of Morris aforesaid in the county of Morris aforesaid and within the jurisdiction of this court, unlawfully and wickedly did willfully blaspheme the Holy name of God by contumeliously reproaching his Being and Providence and by contumeliously reproaching Jesus Christ, and the Holy Word of God, that is the canonical scriptures contained in the Old and New Testaments, and by profane scoffing at and exposing them to contempt and ridicule, in that he the said Charles B. Reynolds did then and there publish, circulate and distribute a certain scandalous impious and blasphemous printed document entitles "Blasphemy and the Bible by Charles B. Reynolds" in which there were and are contained among other things certain scandalous, impious, and blasphemous matters and things to the tenor and effect following…

[the remainder of the Morristown indictment is identical to the Boonton indictment]

(signed) Willard W. Cutler
Prosecutor of Morris County[102]

The second indictment by the Grand Jury for Morris County was not based on Reynolds' arrest and blasphemy charge in Boonton. There were two charges of blasphemy cited in the second indictment and both were based solely upon the pamphlet that Reynolds distributed in Morristown.[103]

---

[102] Morris Oyer and Terminer. May Term 1887 *The State v. Charles B. Reynolds Indictment.* Signed by Willard W. Cutler. Filed May 6, 1887 by Clerk M. S. Condit, 5 pp. (typed-upper case, double spaced) Text of indictment (photocopy) obtained from Mr. David Mitros , Archivist, Morris County Heritage Commission, P. O. Box 900, Morristown, New Jersey 07963-0900.

[103] The text of both indictments are virtually identical. Only the dates and locations are different.

Blasphemy Trial

The editor of *The Truth Seeker*, E. M. MacDonald, arranged for famous trial attorney, lecturer and freethinker, Col. Robert Ingersoll, to defend Charles Reynolds. Ingersoll was undoubtedly the leading voice in the American freethought movement during the nineteenth century. Moreover, he was the President of the American Secular Union and Reynolds was the chair of the Executive Committee so they were well acquainted and held similar views about religion. As a result, it was inevitable that Ingersoll would agree to represent Reynolds at his blasphemy trial. In fact, Ingersoll intended to use the trial as another platform to argue his case for the separation of church and state.

Robert G. Ingersoll was born in 1833 in Dresden, New York. His father preached as a Congregational and, later, a Presbyterian minister. Ingersoll worked briefly as a school teacher then read law and was admitted to the bar. In 1855, he and his brother Ebon Ingersoll started a law practice in Shawneetown, Illinois. Later, they moved their practice to Peoria. Ingersoll ran as a candidate for Congress as a Democrat in 1860 but lost the election.[104]

In 1861, Ingersoll entered the U.S. Army. He was given the rank of Colonel and command of the 11th Regiment of the Illinois Volunteer Cavalry. Colonel Ingersoll participated in the bloody battle of Shiloh in 1862. On December 17, 1862, Col. Ingersoll, with a mixed force of 800 including cavalry from the 11th Illinois, 2nd West Tennessee and 5th Ohio as well as a battery of cannon

---

[104] C. H. Cramer. *Royal Bob: The Life of Robert G. Ingersoll* New York: The Bobbs-Merrill Company, Inc. (1952), Ch. II-III.

from the 14th Indiana, was defeated by 2,500 Confederate cavalry under the command of Gen. Nathan Bedford Forrest. Col. Ingersoll was captured but paroled after a few days – a common practice during the Civil War.

A correspondent of the Chicago *Times* gives the following account of Col. Robert G. Ingersoll's capture by Gen. Forrest: Ingersoll was reconnoitering with a small detachment and came upon a nest of sharpshooters greatly outnumbering them. The first indication of danger was that Ingersoll noticed a "butternut" drawing a bead on him. With the readiness that has saved him from defeat in many a law suit he cried out: "What do you want to shoot me for? I've been wanting to acknowledge your old confederacy for the last two seconds." The fellow appreciated the joke. Of course he didn't shoot. The squad was lead to headquarters. The joke soon circulated through the camp, and the rebs would flock about the prison-tent curious to catch a glimpse of "that Yank." Forrest treated him very kindly, and when he was exchanged returned to Ingersoll his horse, with a note addressed, "To the man who saved his life by a joke in the face of death."[105]

A short time later, on June 30, 1863, he resigned and returned home.[106] After the Civil War, Ingersoll worked as an attorney and lecturer. He served briefly as Attorney General of Illinois during 1867-1869. In the late 1860s, Ingersoll began the anti-religious lectures and essays that would establish his reputation as the "great agnostic" of his times.[107]

---

[105] *Lowell Daily Citizen* (Lowell, MA), January 12, 1877, Issue 6424.
[106] C. H. Cramer. *Royal Bob: The Life of Robert G. Ingersoll* New York: The Bobbs-Merrill Company, Inc. (1952), Ch. IV.
[107] Another famous trial attorney and skeptic, Clarence S. Darrow (1857-1938) found Col. Ingersoll to be a model public speaker who had no peers in his lifetime.

"No one ever really spoke as he did; one could analyze Ingersoll's speeches if not imitate them; every sentence was rhythmical and in prose; as much so as the best of Keats or Robert Burns, or Housman in poetry. There was never so much as a word awry. There were the exact number of feet to fit the prose measure,

It was the lecture called "The Gods," which made Ingersoll famous as an agnostic overnight. This brilliant and audacious oration created a sensation, and was widely discussed by press and pulpit. The bold paraphrase of Alexander Pope, "an honest God is the noblest work of man," is perhaps the most celebrated line in all of Ingersoll's lectures. The Colonel did not mean this to be taken literally, for he did not believe that an honest God is the noblest work of man. On the contrary, in his opinion, god-manufacturing was one of the least important and useful of human occupations. What he did mean was that man has always made his God or gods in his own image; that the conception of God has developed as man himself has developed, and that in order to have an honest God there must first be honest men. [108]

Ingersoll's final lecture, "What is Religion?" was delivered during a meeting of the American Free Religions Association in Boston, Massachusetts on April 2, 1899.[109]

Ingersoll was well known for standing ideas on their heads and this usually had a lasting impact on those hearing his lectures. For example, he argued that a person's religion is dependent upon where the person was born.

---

and the subject. Evidently most of his speeches were accurately prepared; and, above all, he had something to say. I heard him twice, and with everyone in the audience I was entranced. Along with the other aspiring lawyers I tried to adopt his style, and I think I succeeded fairly well, at that time, but it was not Ingersoll. Others tried, too, but most of them failed, so far as I knew. I have found a few who mastered his form of expression, but they lacked what Ingersoll never lacked, and that was something worth saying." Clarence Darrow. *The Story of My Life* New York: Grosset & Dunlap (1932) [Grosset's Universal Library], p. 381.

[108] Eva Ingersoll Wakefield. *The Letters of Robert G. Ingersoll* Westport, CT: Greenwood Press, Publishers (1973), p. 51. [Originally published, New York: Philosophical Library (1951)]. Eva Ingersoll Wakefield was a granddaughter of Col. Robert G. Ingersoll.

[109] Ibid., p. 57.

List of Illustrations

All illustrations from *The Truth Seeker* used with the permission of the editor. The photograph of the U. S. Hotel used with the permission of the Boonton Historical Society.

C. B. Reynolds' Tent
Source: *The Truth Seeker Annual* [1886]

“Casting pearls before swine” – C. B. Reynolds in Boonton, New Jersey
Source: *The Truth Seeker* (cover) [Vol. 13, No. 36, September 4, 1886]

United States Hotel in Boonton, New Jersey
Source: Boonton Historical Society

Charles B. Reynolds
Source: *The Truth Seeker* [1886]

[Ingersoll] declared that our beliefs, religious or otherwise, are chiefly determined by the place and period in which we happen to be born – by heredity, environment, education, and many other preconditioning factors. If we had been inhabitants of some primitive part of the world, we would probably have believed in other 'sacred scriptures'; "we might have believed in a God with three heads instead of three Gods with one head as we do now," argued Ingersoll, the incorrigible.[110]

There is no doubt that Ingersoll had a gift for turning a phrase. For instance, he made the following observation about whether the Bible was God's holy word.

(I)f the Bible is true, it does not need to be inspired. If it is true, it makes no difference whether it was written by a man or a god.[111]

Also, Ingersoll had a talent for rendering Bible stories absurd with a technique referred to as *reductio ad absurdum.*[112] For example, Ingersoll gave the following account of loading animals on Noah's ark before the Deluge.

---

[110] Ibid., pp.95-96. This is a humorous reference to the Christian doctrine of the "trinity." Another reference to the trinity: "Ingersoll did not believe in divine revelation, but he did believe in the secular revelations of reason, observation and experience – the Holy Trinity of Science." (p. 221).

[111] Ibid., p. 228. Ingersoll was very fond of quoting from Thomas Paine's *The Age of Reason.* Their anti-religious views were very similar.

I do not believe in the creed professed by the Jewish Church, by the Roman Church, by the Greek Church, by the Turkish Church, by the Protestant Church, nor by any church that I know of. My own mind is my own church.

Thomas Paine. *The Age of Reason* Secaucus, New Jersey: Citadel Press (1974), p. 50. [Orig. published as *The Age of Reason: Being an Investigation of True and Fabulous Theology* (1794)]

[112] A Latin phrase that translates,"reduction to absurdity." It means the refutation of a proposition by demonstrating that the logical conclusion is preposterous. *The Random House Dictionary of the English Language*, Jess Stein (ed.), New York: Random House (1973).

Some of the creeping things must have started for the ark just as soon as they were made, and kept up a steady jog for sixteen hundred years...Two sloths had to make the journey from South America. These creatures cannot travel to exceed three rods a day. At this rate, they would make a mile in about a hundred days. They must have gone about six thousand five hundred miles to reach the ark. Supposing them to have traveled by a reasonably direct route, in order to complete the journey before Noah hauled in the plank, they must have started several years before the world was created..."[113]

Finally, Ingersoll was well aware that his opponents would attack his character if they failed to best him in public debates. He commented on this to the Editor of the Duluth Tribune in a letter dated January 3, 1882.

...As they could not answer my arguments, they did the next best thing – they attacked me...Of course my reputation has nothing to do with the question, one way or the other. Admitting that I am the worst man in the world, still there is some doubt about the general deluge. If it should be proved that I am the unfortunate possessor of all the vices, still some people might have their doubt about the whale's having swallowed Jonah. And should I be so unfortunate as to die in the penitentiary, even after that, some folks might say that the doctrine of the trinity was mathematically absurd.[114]

The blasphemy trial of Charles B. Reynolds commenced at 11:00 a.m. on Thursday, May 19, 1887 in the Court of Common Pleas for Morris County, New Jersey. The trial had been much anticipated by local residents and the newspapers because it was the first trial for blasphemy in New Jersey since the statute was enacted during colonial times. In addition, local clergy had been very vocal in their criticism of Reynolds and his attorney, the notorious agnostic, Col. Robert G. Ingersoll. The public benches inside the courtroom were

---

[113] Ibid., pp. 228-229. Here, Ingersoll pokes fun at both the story of Noah's ark and the Christian doctrine that Creation was as recent as 4,000 BC. One "rod" is a unit of measure equivalent to 5-1/2 yards. There are 320 rods in one mile.

[114] Ibid., pp. 250-251.

filled and an overflow crowd waited outside hours before Col. Ingersoll and his clerk arrived by train from New York City.

For six months no topic was so interesting to the public as this. It monopolized attention at the stores, and became a fruitful subject of gossip in social and church circles. Under such circumstances it was to be expected that everybody who could spare the time would go to court yesterday. Lines of people began to climb the Court House hill early in the morning. At the hour of opening court the room set apart for the trial was packed, and distaffs had to be stationed at the foot of the stairs to keep back those who were not early enough. From 9:30 until 11 o'clock the crowd inside talked of blasphemy in all the phases suggested by this case, and the outsiders waited patiently on the lawn and steps and along the dusty approaches to the gray building.[115]

Col. Ingersoll arrived at the Court House by hansom cab along with his associate, R. H. Griffin, and his stenographer, I. N. Baker.[116] The trial was heard by Francis Child[117], presiding judge, as well as DeWitt C. Quimby and Charles H. Munson, who were both lay judges. "The deputy clerk was Dan Vorhees and the

---

[115] "On Trial for Blasphemy: Col. Ingersoll's Defense of Charles B. Reynolds" *New York Times* Friday, May 20, 1887, p. 8.

[116] "Slumbering but Still Alive, Was Law in Famous Blasphemy Case" *Newark Evening News* Saturday, January 3, 1925. Col. Ingersoll published the stenographic report of his closing argument to the jury. Robert G. Ingersoll. *Trial of C. B. Reynolds for Blasphemy at Morristown, N.J., May 19th and 20th, 1887* New York: C. P. Farrell (1888).

[117] "Convicted and Fined" *The Truth Seeker* May 28, 1887 Vol. 14, No. 22, p. 344. According to his obituary, Francis Child was born May 7, 1842 in Morristown, N.J. He enlisted in the 33rd New York Volunteer Infantry at the start of the Civil War and mustered out as a 1st lieutenant at the conclusion. Following the war, he studied law and was admitted to the bar in 1866. He was appointed judge of the common pleas court of Morris County in 1877 and resigned in 1897. He practiced law with his son, Francis Child Jr., in Newark until he died at age 72 from pneumonia.

crier was William Beers."[118] After Col. Ingersoll was seated, Judge Child ordered the court clerk to impanel the jury and he cautioned the spectators to keep quiet.[119]

It only took about five minutes to seat the first five jurors. Then, Col. Ingersoll asked Judge Child about challenges and was informed that the defense was allowed six peremptory challenges but must challenge before the jurors were seated. In addition, Judge Child allowed that a juror could be challenged if he was unable to change his opinion despite the evidence presented.[120]

> There were little snakes of prejudice, as Colonel Ingersoll put it, lurking in the minds of all of them, but the judge held that that made no difference so long as they thought they could acquit Mr. Reynolds providing the evidence showed that he had not distributed the pamphlets in Morristown.[121]

Col. Ingersoll persuaded Judge Child to permit him to re-examine the five seated jurors and he exercised peremptory challenges against two jurors who were Presbyterians. They were excused.[122] Col. Ingersoll continued to examine the prospective jurors. He asked each juror if he was prejudiced. One juror replied that

---

[118] Ibid.

[119] "On Trial for Blasphemy: Col. Ingersoll's Defense of Charles B. Reynolds" *New York Times* Friday, May 20, 1887, p. 8.

[120] Ibid.

[121] Reynolds was being tried on the charges in the second indictment that he committed blasphemy in Morristown. At the conclusion of the trial, Prosecutor Willard W. Cutler stated that he would not submit the first indictment for trial since Reynolds had been convicted on the second indictment. He also explained that Judge Child had been lenient in sentencing Reynolds because the law against blasphemy had never been prosecuted. "Jersey Law Triumphant: Reynolds Found Guilty of Blasphemy" *New York Times* May 21, 1887, p. 8.

[122] "On Trial for Blasphemy: Col. Ingersoll's Defense of Charles B. Reynolds" *New York Times* Friday, May 20, 1887, p. 8

he didn't know what the word meant. Col. Ingersoll explained.

I may not define the word legally, but my own idea is that a man is prejudiced when he has made up his mind on a case without knowing anything about it.[123]

Eventually, after 20 prospective jurors had been examined and the defense had used five preemptory challenges, a jury of twelve men was sworn.[124] The jury consisted of the following[125]:

Jacob Ogden	Methodist	New Vernon
Louis Bowen	no church	Green Village
Andrew B. Coghlan	Catholic	Morristown
Paul H. Mandeville	religion not asked	Morristown
George Schuyler	religion not asked	Morris Plains
Michael Rourke	Catholic	Mount Vernon
Eugene Buchanan	Methodist	Dover
Leon De Hart	religion not asked	Madison
Horace L. Donovan	religion not asked	Dover
Lemuel E. Pearson	religion not asked	Morristown
Benjamin Flaherty	Catholic	-
John McTiernan	Catholic	Madison

After the jury was sworn, Prosecutor Willard W. Cutler advised the court that the state would try Reynolds on the indictment for blasphemy in Morristown, New

---

[123] Ibid.

[124] Ibid. The jury was comprised of all men because women were not allowed to serve as jurors.

[125] Ibid. There is some disagreement among reported accounts at the time of the trial appearing in the *New York Times* and *The Truth Seeker*. However, it seems evident that this was due primarily to errors in recording or spelling the names. For example, these differences exist between the *New York Times* and (*The Truth Seeker*): Bowen (Boing), Coghlan (Cogan), Donovan (Dunham), and Pearson (Pierson). I have relied on the *New York Times* account since it was not a party to the proceedings and its reporting, in all other respects, appears to be accurate.

Jersey. Cutler gave a brief, one minute, opening statement to the effect that Reynolds was accused of distributing a blasphemous pamphlet. Next, he spent two hours examining 16 townspeople who claimed to have been given the pamphlets by Reynolds.[126]

Col. Ingersoll questioned the religious witnesses to find any who would admit to having read the pamphlet, *Blasphemy and the Bible*, but without success. Presumably, he intended to ask these witnesses whether they believed that the pamphlet was blasphemous, by merely repeating Bible stories, and thereby effectively place the Bible on trial instead of Reynolds. In any case, no witness would admit to having read the pamphlet. Ingersoll conducted no further cross-examination.[127]

During the witness testimony, there was a short disruption by a man in the gallery. The account by the reporter from the *New York Times* was suitably droll to match the general tone of the coverage of the trial by that newspaper.

> As one of the witnesses stepped aside a man in the audience, whose brain seemed to have been dazed by too much cogitation or blasphemy, rose, and, with a feeble wave of his hat, said: "Thr' cheers fo' Bob Ing'sul." Judge Child sternly handed him over to the Sheriff, to whom the enthusiast explained that he thought he was at a meeting and had a right to cheer.[128]

The witnesses included:

John W. Babbitt	constable
Winfield West	bill poster
Thomas Cleary	
Benjamin McLean	

---

[126] Ibid.
[127] Ibid.
[128] Ibid.

Matthew Lowe
Mr. Dutton
George L. Clark
David L. Fox
Charles Thursten
Lewis Armstrong
[District Attorney Willard W. Cutler] then called as witness John W. Babbitt, a constable of the court, who was armed with a copy of the pamphlet, which he swore he had religiously preserved locked up in his bookcase ever since it was given to him by Mr. Reynolds in person.[129]

After the witness testimony for the prosecution, Cutler rested his case and Col. Ingersoll asked the court for a recess.

"I don't know that I shall have any witnesses one way or the other," Col. Ingersoll said, rising to suggest a recess. Perhaps after dinner I may feel like making a few remarks.
"There will be great disappointment if you don't," Judge Child responded, in a tone that meant a word for himself as well as for the other listeners. The spectators nodded approval to this sentiment.[130]

It was a hot summer afternoon and the audience was "spell-bound."[131] The *New York Times* reported that, "...court reassembled with an attendance so much larger than that of the morning that the overflow packed the

---

[129] "Convicted and Fined" *The Truth Seeker* Vol. 14, No. 22, May 28, 1887, p. 344. Note the sarcasm in the term, "religiously preserved."
[130] "On Trial for Blasphemy" *New York Times*, Friday, May 20, 1887, p. 8. Col. Ingersoll presumably wanted to delay the start of his prepared remarks to the jury, and the spectators, until after lunch so its impact wasn't diminished by an interruption. Col. Ingersoll and Judge Child were both very aware that the large gathering of spectators was there precisely to hear Ingersoll's comments because he was a well-known lecturer and passionate about the subject of religious interference with free speech rights.
[131] "Convicted and Fined" *The Truth Seeker* Vol. 14, No. 22, May 28, 1887, p. 344.

halls and stairways..."[132] Col. Ingersoll began his closing statement to the jury at 2:00 p.m. on Thursday, May 19, 1887, and he spoke until 4:20 p.m. whereupon the judge adjourned the court until the next morning.[133] Ingersoll continued his address at 9:30 a.m. and concluded at 10:45 a.m. on May 20, 1887 [134] The text of Ingersoll's closing statement was recorded by his stenographer and published in full the following year.[135]

When Ingersoll began his closing statement, he immediately summed his defense as follows:

> Gentlemen of the Jury: I regard this as one of the most important cases that can be submitted to a jury....It involves the freedom of speech, the intellectual liberty of every citizen of New Jersey. The question to be tried by you is whether a man has the right to express his honest thought...[136]

Ingersoll turned first to the question of whether individuals had any control over their thoughts or beliefs. He argued that God would have created all men to think the same if he wished that.

> It seems to me that if there is some infinite being who wants us to think alike, he would have made us alike. Why did he not do so? Why did he make your brain [*presumably pointing to a member of the jury*] so that you could not by any possibility be a Methodist? Why did he make yours [*pointing to another*] so that you could not be a Catholic? And why did he make the brain of another so that he

---

[132] "On Trial for Blasphemy" *New York Times*, Friday, May 20, 1887, p. 8.
[133] Ibid.
[134] "Convicted and Fined" *The Truth Seeker* Vol. 14, No. 22, May 28, 1887, p. 344-345.
[135] Robert G. Ingersoll. *Trial of C.B. Reynolds for Blasphemy at Morristown, N.J., May 19th and 20th, 1887* New York City: C. P. Farrell (1888), 84 pp.
[136] Ibid., p.3.

is an unbeliever – why the brain of another so that he became a Mohammedan – if he wanted us all to believe alike?[137]

Col. Ingersoll was seeking to demonstrate that God intended people to think differently so it could not be a crime to be an unbeliever and that the constitutional right of free speech permitted each to voice their honest thoughts. It was Ingersoll's plan to convince the jury that the trial was not about blasphemy but, rather, about the constitutional right of free speech which rendered the state's blasphemy law unenforceable.

Next, Col. Ingersoll moved on to define blasphemy and he asserted that it all depended upon where in the world you happened to live.

We send missionaries to other countries. What for? To tell them that their religion is false, that their Gods are myths and monsters, that their Saviours and apostles were imposters, and that our religion is true. You send a man from Morristown – a Presbyterian, over to Turkey. He goes there, and he tells the Mohammedans – and he has it in a pamphlet and he distributes it – that the Koran is a lie, that Mohammet was not a prophet of God,[*a not so subtle reference to Reynold's distribution of his pamphlet*]...Then what would the Turks do? Suppose the Turks had a law like this statute in New Jersey. They would put the Morristown missionary in jail, and he would send home word, and then what would the people of Morristown say? Honestly – what do you think they would say? They would say, "Why look at these poor heathen wretches. We sent a man over there armed with the truth, and yet they were so blinded by their idolatrous religion, so steeped in superstition, that they actually put that man in prison"... Now let us turn the tables. A gentleman comes from Turkey to Morristown. He has got a pamphlet. He says, "The Koran is the inspired book, Mohammed is the real prophet, your bible is

---

137 Ibid., pp. 6-7. Here, Col. Ingersoll makes an argument based upon determinism and ignores the doctrine of "free will" which is crucial to a Christian's understanding of sin.

false and your Saviour simply a myth." Thereupon the Morristown people put him in jail.[138]

This story provided Col. Ingersoll with his next point – that the trial, instead of quieting blasphemous speech, was actually spreading it to a larger audience.

Here comes a man into your town and circulates a pamphlet. Now if they had just kept still, very few would ever have heard of it. That would have been the end. The diameter of the echo would have been a few thousand feet. But in order to stop the discussion of that question, they indicted this man, and that question has been more discussed in this country since this indictment than all the discussions put together since New Jersey was first granted to Charles the Second's dearest brother James, the Duke of York. And what else? A trial here that is to be reported and published all over the United States, a trial that will give Mr. Reynolds a congregation of fifty millions of people. And yet this was done for the purpose of stopping a discussion of this subject.[139]

Moreover, Ingersoll said, you can't put an idea in jail.

Suppose that we put Mr. Reynolds in jail. The argument has not been sent to jail. That is still going the rounds, free as the winds. Suppose you keep him at hard labor a year – all the time he is there hundreds and thousands of people will be reading some account, or some fragment, of this trial. There is the trouble. If you could only imprison a thought, then intellectual tyranny might succeed.[140]

Following this overview of his free speech argument, Col. Ingersoll proceeded to examine the blasphemy statute phrase by phrase. His purpose was to demonstrate that the statute was absurd on its face and that is was unenforceable in any case.

---

[138] Robert G. Ingersoll. *Trial of C.B. Reynolds for Blasphemy at Morristown, N.J., May 19th and 20th, 1887* New York City: C. P. Farrell (1888), pp. 13-14.
[139] Ibid., pp. 14-15.
[140] Ibid., p. 15.

> Nobody roused the [colonial era blasphemy] statute until the defendant in this case went to Boonton, and there made a speech in which he gave his honest thought , and the people not having an argument handy, threw stones. Thereupon Mr. Reynolds, the defendant, published a pamphlet on Blasphemy and in it gave a photograph of the Boonton Christians. That is his offence. Now let us read this infamous statute:
> "*If any person shall willfully blaspheme the holy name of God by denying, cursing, or contumeliously reproaching his being*" -
> I want to say right here – many a man has cursed the God of another man. The Catholics have cursed the God of the Protestant. The Presbyterians have cursed the God of the Catholics – charged them with idolatry – cursed their images, laughed at their ceremonies. And these compliments have been interchanged between all the religions of the world. But I say here to-day that no man, unless a raving maniac, ever cursed the God in whom he believed. ….[T]here was time when you could have cursed Zeus, the god of the Greeks, and like Socrates, they would have compelled you to drink hemlock. Yet now everybody can curse this god. Why? Is the god dead? No. He is just as alive as he ever was. Then what has happened? The Greeks have passed away. That is all. So in all our churches here. Whenever a Church is in the minority it clamors for free speech. When it gets in the majority, no. I do not believe the history of the world will show that any orthodox Church when in the majority ever had the courage to face the free lips of the world. It sends for a constable. And is it not wonderful that they should do this when they preach the gospel of universal forgiveness – when they say, "if a man strike you on one cheek turn to him the other also" – but if he laughs at your religion, put him in the penitentiary.[141]

Here, Col. Ingersoll, shows that even Christians blaspheme each other's churches and that religions all over the world are in conflict. He argues that Reynolds didn't believe in the Christian religion that he mocked any more than Presbyterians believe in Catholicism. With some mischief, he proceeds to cite the Christian law that requires believers to forgive an offender which

---

[141] Robert G. Ingersoll. *Trial of C.B. Reynolds for Blasphemy at Morristown, N.J., May 19th and 20th, 1887* New York City: C. P. Farrell (1888), pp. 21-23.

stands in stark contrast to the trial for blasphemy in Morristown.

Let us read a little further:
"- *Or by cursing or contumeliously reproaching Jesus Christ.*"
Why, whoever did, since the poor man, or the poor God, was crucified? How did they come to crucify him? Because they did not believe in free speech in Jerusalem. How else? Because there was a law against blasphemy in Jerusalem – a law exactly like this.[142]

Col. Ingersoll argued that Jesus himself was a victim of blasphemy laws. It is ironic that Col. Ingersoll, in his closing statement, made many blasphemous remarks and, like Reynolds, he used the words of the Bible to make his points.

Let me read you another line from this ignorant statute:-
"*Or the Christian religion.*"
Well, what is the Christian religion? "If you scoff at the Christian religion – if you curse the Christian religion." Well what is it? Gentlemen, you hear Presbyterians every day attack the Catholic Church. Is that the Christian religion? The Catholic believes it is the Christian religion, and you have to admit that it is the oldest one, and then the Catholics turn around and scoff at the Protestants. Is that the Christian religion? If so, every Christian religion has been cursed by every other Christian religion. Is not that an absurd and foolish statute?[143]

Again, Col. Ingersoll returns to his argument that if Reynolds were guilty of blasphemy for attacking the Catholics, then the Presbyterians – in the jury and the audience – were equally guilty.

"*The Holy Scriptures.*"
Are they holy? Must a man be honest? Has he the right to be sincere? There are thousands of things in the Scriptures that everybody believes. Everybody believes the Scriptures are right

---

[142] Ibid., pp. 23-24.
[143] Robert G. Ingersoll. *Trial of C.B. Reynolds for Blasphemy at Morristown, N.J., May 19th and 20th, 1887*, op. cit., p. 26.

when they say, "Thou shalt not steal" – everybody. And when they say "Give good measure, heaped up and running over," everybody says, "Good!" So when they say "Love your neighbor," everybody applauds that. Suppose a man believes that, and practices it, does it make any difference whether he believes in the flood or not? Is that of any importance? Whether a man built an ark or not – does that make the slightest difference? A man might deny it and yet be a very good man. Another might believe it and be a very mean man. Could it now, by any possibility, make a man a good father, a good husband, a good citizen?[144]

In these comments, Col. Ingersoll side steps the issue of whether the Holy Scriptures are holy and, instead, questions whether belief in some of the stories in the Bible affects whether a man is good. His intent, clearly, was to argue that Reynolds disbelief in these stories didn't make him a bad man.

"*Or by profane scoffing expose them to ridicule.*"
Think of such a law as that, passed under a Constitution that says, "No law shall abridge the liberty of speech." But you must not ridicule the Scriptures. Did anybody ever dream of passing a law to protect Shakespeare from being laughed at? Did anybody ever think of such a thing? Did anybody ever want any legislative enactment to keep people from holding Robert Burns in contempt? The songs of Burns will be sung as long as there is love in the human heart. Do we need to protect him from ridicule by a statute? Does he need assistance from New Jersey? Is any statute needed to keep Euclid from being laughed at in this neighborhood? And is it possible that a work written by an infinite being has to be protected by a legislature? Is it possible that a book cannot be written by a God so that it will not excite the laughter of the human race?[145]

Col. Ingersoll returns to his argument about free speech. But, here he asks why the Scriptures, if they were authored by God, need to be protected from human criticism by laws.

---

[144] Ibid., p. 28.
[145] Robert G. Ingersoll. *Trial of C.B. Reynolds for Blasphemy at Morristown, N.J., May 19th and 20th, 1887*, op. cit., pp. 30-31.

Let us read another clause:-
"*And every person so offending shall, on conviction, be fined not exceeding two hundred dollars, or imprisoned at hard labor not exceeding twelve months, or both.*"
I want you to remember that this statute was passed in England hundreds of years ago – just in that language. The punishment, however, has been somewhat changed. In the good old days when the king sat on the throne …it was "All his goods shall be confiscated; his tongue shall be bored with a hot iron, and upon his forehead he shall be branded with the letter B; and for the second offence he shall suffer death by burning." Those were the good old days when people maintained the orthodox religion in all its purity and in all its ferocity.[146]

Finally, Col. Ingersoll sought to demonstrate that the New Jersey blasphemy law was a holdover from the "good old days" of religious persecution. It is certain that the reference to England reminded the jurors that their ancestors left Europe, in large part, for religious freedom. Col. Ingersoll concludes that "Now this persecution differs only in degree from the infamies of the olden time."[147]

By this time, Col. Ingersoll was nearly half-way through his closing statement and he changed the focus to pose a series of questions to the jury. His intention was to return to his opening remarks that the blasphemy statute was unconstitutional.

The first question for you, gentlemen, to decide in this case is: Is this statute constitutional? Is this statute in harmony with that part of the [New Jersey] Constitution of 1844 which says: "The liberty of speech shall not be abridged.?" That is for you to say. Is this law constitutional, or is it simply an old statute that fell asleep, that was forgotten, that people simply failed to repeal? I believe I can

---

[146] Ibid., pp. 31-32.
[147] Ibid., p. 37.

convince you, if you will think a moment, that our fathers never intended to establish a government like that.[148]

Col. Ingersoll, here, challenges the constitutionality of the blasphemy statute by discussing the religious beliefs of Thomas Jefferson, a founding father who was a deist and disbelieved the stories of miracles in the New Testament while admiring the moral teachings of Jesus.[149] In 1820, Thomas Jefferson cut out the references to supernatural events in the New Testament and pasted together the remainder in a new volume that was titled, *The Life and Morals of Jesus*.[150] In a long letter to John Adams, dated October 12, 1813, Thomas Jefferson gave vent to his true feeling about religious dogmaticism and the evils it caused.

In extracting the pure principles which [Jesus] taught, we should have to strip off the artificial vestments in which they have been muffled by priests, who have travestied them into various forms, as instruments of riches and power to them. We must dismiss the Platonists and Plotinists, the Stagyrites and Gamalielites, the Eclectics the Gnostics and Scholastics their essences and emanations, their Logos and Demi-urgos, Aeons and Daemons male and female, with a long train of etc. etc. etc. or, shall I say at once, of Nonsense. We must reduce our volume to the simple evangelists, select, even from them, the very words only of Jesus, paring off the Amphibologisms into which they have been led by forgetting often, or not understanding, what had fallen from him, by giving their own misconceptions as his dicta, and expressing unintelligibly for others

---

[148] Ibid., p. 32.

[149] Ibid., p. 35. "Thomas Jefferson entertained about the same views entertained by the defendant in this case, and he was made President of the United States. He was the author of the Declaration of Independence, founder of the University of Virginia, writer of that clause in the Constitution of that State that made all the citizens equal before the law."

[150] Dickinson W. Adams (ed.). *Jefferson's Extracts from the Gospels: "The Philosophy of Jesus" and "The Life and Morals of Jesus"* Princeton, New Jersey: Princeton University Press (1983) [The Papers of Thomas Jefferson, Second Series], p. 125.

what they had not understood themselves. There will be found remaining the most sublime and benevolent code of morals which has ever been offered to man. I have performed this operation for my own use, by cutting verse by verse out of the printed book, and arranging, the matter which is evidently his, and which is as easily distinguishable as diamonds in a dunghill. The result is an 8vo. of 45 pages of pure and unsophisticated doctrines, such as were professed and acted on by the unlettered apostles, the Apostolic fathers, and the Christians of the 1st century. Their Platonising successors indeed, in aftertimes, in order to legitimate the corruptions which they had incorporated into the doctrines of Jesus, found it necessary to disavow the primitive Christians, who had taken their principles from the mouth of Jesus himself, of his Apostles, and the Fathers contemporary with them.[151]

Next, Col. Ingersoll asks the jury rhetorically whether a man should be judged by his beliefs or his deeds.

A man does not wish to belong to any church. Are you going to judge him? Judge him by the way he treats his wife, his children, his neighbors. Does he pay his debts? Does he tell the truth? Does he help the poor? Has he got a heart that melts when he hears grief's story? That is the way to judge him. I don't care what he thinks about…the flood, about bibles or gods. When some poor mother is found wandering in the street with a babe at her breast, does he quote Scripture, or hunt for his pocket-book? That is the way to judge. And suppose he does not believe in any bible whatever? If Christianity is true, that is his misfortune, and everybody should pity the poor wretch that is going down the hill. Why kick him? You will get your revenge on him through all eternity – is not that enough?[152]

He follows with the comment that the religious beliefs of people aren't choices anyway but simply inherited from parents like eye color. Ironically, Col. Ingersoll delivered his message in the same manner as the secular sermons of his client, Reynolds, and not different than ministers preach to their congregations.

---

[151] Ibid., p.352.

[152] Robert G. Ingersoll. *Trial of C.B. Reynolds for Blasphemy at Morristown, N.J., May 19th and 20th, 1887*, op. cit., p.38.

So I say, let us judge each other by our actions, not by theories, not by what we happen to believe - because that depends very much on where we were born. If you had been born in Turkey, you probably would have been a Mohammedan. If I had been born among the Hindoos, I might have been a Buddhist – I can't tell.[153]

Col. Ingersoll continues by concluding that blasphemy laws, if enforced, would have prevented human knowledge of science and, even, prevented the writing of books.[154]

At this point in his closing statement, Col. Ingersoll began a detailed examination of the charges in the indictment. He discussed each line in turn to challenge its truth.

Now let us see the frightful things that this man, the defendant in this case, has done. Let me read the charges against him as set out in this indictment. I shall insist that this statute does not cover any publication – that it covers simply speech – not in writing, not in book or pamphlet. Let us see:

"This bible describes God as so loving that he drowned the whole world in his mad fury."
Well, the great question about that is, is it true? Does the bible describe God as having drowned the whole world with the exception of eight people? Does it, or does it not? I don't know whether there is anybody in this country who has really read the bible, but I believe the story of the flood is there. It does say that God destroyed all flesh, and that he did so because he was angry. He says so himself, if the bible be true.[155]

According to Col. Ingersoll, Reynolds merely retold a story from the Bible which Christians believe is true.

---

[153] Ibid., p. 39.
[154] Ibid., p. 41. "[Astronomy] is contrary to the bible, and for asserting the truth you become a criminal." This is an allusion to the trial of Galileo by the Inquisition for asserting that the earth revolves about the sun rather than the contrary.
[155] Ibid., pp. 44-45.

His intent was to convince the jury that if Reynolds was guilty of blasphemy then the Bible too must be found blasphemous. This argument was a key part of the defense.

The defendant has simply repeated what is in the bible. The bible says that God is loving, and says that he drowned the world, and that he was angry. Is it blasphemy to quote from the "sacred Scriptures?"[156]

Col. Ingersoll took this idea a step further by drawing conclusions from the flood story in the Bible.

"Because it was so much worse than he, knowing all things, ever supposed it could be."

If God knows all things, he must have known at the time he made them that he was going to drown them. Is it likely that a being of infinite wisdom would deliberately do what he knew he must undo? Is it blasphemy to ask that question? Have you a right to think about it at all? If you have, you have the right to tell somebody what you think – if not, you have no right to discuss it, no right to think about it. All you have to do is to read it and believe it – to open your mouth like a young robin, and swallow – worms or shingle nails – no matter which.[157]

This argument links the concepts of biblical criticism and free speech. The foundation of the defense is that Reynolds did not engage in blasphemy but, rather, free speech.

"An all-wise, unchangeable God, who got out of patience with a world which was just what his own stupid blundering had made it, knew no better way out of the muddle than to destroy it by drowning!"

Is that true? Was not the world exactly as God made it? Certainly. Did he not, if the bible is true, drown the people? He did. Did he

[156] Ibid., p. 45.
[157] Ibid., p. 45.

know he would drown them when he made them? He did. Did he know they ought to be drowned when they were made? He did. Where, then, is the blasphemy in saying so?[158]

Here, Col. Ingersoll introduces a profound new argument. He suggests that it may be incompatible to believe in God and in the Bible. Specifically, he states the following.

If there be a good God, the story is not true. If there be a wise God, the story is not true. Ought an honest man to be sent to the penitentiary for simply telling the truth?[159]

He continues with his examination of the statements of Reynolds contained in the indictment.

"And now he will raise the mischief with them [people]; that his anger burns like hell."

That is true. The bible says of God – "My anger burns to the lowest hell." And that is all that the defendant says. Every word of it is in the bible. He simply does not believe it – and for that reason is a "blasphemer."[160]

Col. Ingersoll went on to state that Reynolds didn't say anything that wasn't in the bible and, "not a word that has not been said in hundreds of pulpits in the Christian world."[161]

The Old Testament records for our instruction in morals the most foul and bestial instances of fornication, incest, and polygamy, perpetrated by God's own saints, and the New Testament indorses these lecherous wretches as examples for all good Christians to follow."

* * *

---

[158] Robert G. Ingersoll. *Trial of C.B. Reynolds for Blasphemy at Morristown, N.J., May 19th and 20th, 1887*, op. cit., pp. 45-46.
[159] Ibid., p. 47.
[160] Ibid., pp. 47-48.
[161] Ibid., p. 48.

We have all heard of Solomon – a gentleman with five or six hundred wives, and three or four hundred other ladies with whom he was acquainted. This is simply what the defendant says. Is there any blasphemy about that? It is only the truth. If Solomon were living in the United States today, we would put him in the penitentiary.

* * *

So it was with David. There are some splendid things about David of course. I admit that, and pay my tribute of respect to his courage – but he happened to have ten or twelve wives too many, so he shut them up, put them in a kind of penitentiary and kept them there till they died. That would not be considered good conduct even in Morristown. You know that. Is it any harm to speak of it?[162]

This brought Col. Ingersoll back to his main theme of liberty of speech. He argues that Reynolds may have said things that conflicted with the religious beliefs of others, and that Reynolds may have made his statements in a disagreeable manner, but that it was an exercise of his constitutional right of free speech.

[Reynolds] had the right to give his honest thought, no matter whether any human being agreed with what he said or not, and no matter whether any other man approved of the manner in which he said these things. I defend his right to speak, whether I believe in what he spoke or not, or in the propriety of saying what he did.[163]

The recent history of trials for atheism and blasphemy in the U.S. and England were reviewed by Col. Ingersoll. He mentioned the George Jacob Holyoake 1843 trial for atheism in England[164] and the Abner Kneeland 1834 trial

---

[162] Ibid., pp. 49-50.

[163] Robert G. Ingersoll. *Trial of C.B. Reynolds for Blasphemy at Morristown, N.J., May 19th and 20th, 1887*, op. cit., p. 51.

[164] See George Jacob Holyoake. *The History of the Last Trial by Jury for Atheism in England: A Fragment of Autobiography, Submitted for the Perusal of Her Majesty's Attorney-General and the British Clergy* London: James Watson (1851) [reprinted by Arno Press & the New York Time (1972)]. See also, Joseph McCabe. *Life and Letters of George Jacob Holyoake* Vol. I London: Watts & Co. (1908)

for blasphemy in Boston. Col. Ingersoll concluded that the absence of any blasphemy cases in the U.S. during the previous half century proved his argument that the blasphemy statute was a relic of the past and obsolete in the modern world.

The case against Kneeland was tried more than fifty years ago, and there has been none since in the New England states; and this case, that we are now trying, is the first ever tried in New Jersey. The fact that it is the first, certifies to my interpretation of the statute. And it also certifies to the toleration and the civilization of the people of this state.

* * *

It is too late to enforce a law like this. Why has it been allowed to slumber? Who obtained this indictment? Were they actuated by good and noble motives? Had they the public weal at heart, or were they simply endeavoring to be revenged upon this defendant? Were they willing to disgrace the State in order that they might punish him?[165]

Finally, Col. Ingersoll summed up his defense for the jury point by point.

First. I claim that the Constitution of New Jersey declares that:

"The liberty of speech shall not be abridged."

Second. That this statute, under which this indictment is found, is unconstitutional, because it does abridge the liberty of speech; it does exactly that which the Constitution emphatically says shall not be done.

Third. I claim, also, that under this law – even if it be constitutional – the words charged in this indictment do not amount to blasphemy, read even in the light, or rather the darkness, of this statute.[166]

The *New York Times* reporter at the trial summarized the legal points that Col. Ingersoll submitted to the Court regarding charges to the jury and the decision by Judge Child.

---

165 Robert G. Ingersoll. *Trial of C.B. Reynolds for Blasphemy at Morristown, N.J., May 19th and 20th, 1887*, op. cit., , pp. 72-73.

166 Ibid., p. 76.

Col. Ingersoll submitted seven requests to charge. He wanted it charged that the law was unconstitutional; that if constitutional, it did not cover a case of distribution of printed matter, but only a case of words spoken; that the jury was to take cognizance only of the words specified in the indictment, and not of the words in the pamphlet or of pictures; that in this case the jury were judges of law as well as fact; that the words quoted were not in the meaning of the definition of blasphemy; that if the jury believe the words to have been not willfully written they must find the defendant not guilty; and that the jury had no right to draw presumptions or inferences because of the neglect of the defendant to testify.

* * *

Judge Child declined to charge any of the requests except that confining the jury to the words stated in the indictment, but as he immediately allowed the jury to take the entire pamphlet to their room with them the defense did not see that they had gained much of a point by the charge.[167]

The *Boston Investigator* reported the request that Col. Ingersoll made to change the charges to the jury somewhat differently.

Col. Ingersoll presented written requests to charge the jury to the following effect: That the law is unconstitutional; that it does not cover the mere distribution of a pamphlet, without any proof as to the authorship of it; that the jury are the judges of the law as well as the facts in such a case, under the constitutional provision as to libel, the indictment alleging a "blasphemous libel"; that the words are not blasphemous under the statute, and that only those parts of the pamphlet must be considered which are quoted in the indictment. Judge Childs refused to charge all except the last of these points.[168]

Col. Ingersoll gave his own instructions to the jury – in anticipation of the judge's instructions to the jury – where he urged the jury to consider only the words of Reynolds contained in the indictment.

---

[167] "Jersey Law Triumphant: Reynolds Found Guilty of Blasphemy" *New York Times* May 21, 1887, p. 8.

[168] "Trial and Conviction of C. B. Reynolds for Blasphemy" *Boston Investigator* May 25, 1887, Issue 7, p. 3.

Do not, I pray you, forget this point. Do not forget that, no matter what the Court may tell you about the law – how good it is or how bad it is – no matter what the Court may instruct you on that subject – do not forget one thing, and that is: that the words charged in the indictment are the only words that you can take into consideration in this case. Remember that, no matter what pictures or cartoons there may be of the gentlemen in Boonton who mobbed this man in the name of universal liberty and love – do not forget that you have no right to take one word into account except the exact words set out in this indictment – that is to say, the words that I have read to you: upon this point the Court will instruct you that you have nothing to do with any other line in that pamphlet; and I now claim, that should the Court instruct you that the statute is constitutional, still I insist that the words set out in this indictment do not amount to blasphemy. There is still another point. This statute says: "Whoever shall willfully speak against." Now, in this case, you must find that the defendant "willfully" did so and so – that is to say that he made the statements attributed to him knowing that they were not true. If you believe that he was honest in what he said, then this statute does not touch him.[169]

The defense defines "willfully" by giving it the meaning "dishonestly." The prosecutor and judge clearly give it a different meaning so that it refers to "intentionally" rather than accidentally or incidentally committing the act. Col. Ingersoll wishes to make the point that, if Reynolds believed what he wrote to be true, then his motive in writing the pamphlet was not to libel God or the Christian religion. Moreover, if he believed what he wrote to be drawn directly from the Bible, then how could it be a crime to state what Christians believe to be true?

In addition to the foregoing, Col. Ingersoll reminds the jury that the New Jersey blasphemy statute was never applied since it was adopted during the colonial era in

---

[169] Robert G. Ingersoll. *Trial of C.B. Reynolds for Blasphemy at Morristown, N.J., May 19th and 20th, 1887*, op. cit., pp. 76-77.

the year 1664. The implication was that the people of New Jersey didn't support the blasphemy statute and that it was obsolete. He questioned the motives of the persons who sought the indictment. Col. Ingersoll also challenged the evidence against the defendant.

Is there any evidence – has there been any – to show that the defendant was not absolutely candid in the expression of his opinions? Is there one particle of evidence tending to show that he is not a perfectly honest and sincere man? Did the prosecution have the courage to attack his reputation? No. The State has simply proved to you that he circulated that pamphlet – that is all.[170]

In an appeal to their own experience with persecution by other religious sects, Col. Ingersoll spoke directly to the Methodists and Catholics on the jury.

There may be among you some Methodists. If so, they have read the history of their Church, and they know that when it was in the minority it was persecuted, and they know that they cannot read the history of that persecution without becoming indignant. They know that the early Methodists were denounced as heretics, as ranters, as ignorant pretenders. There are also on this jury Catholics, and they know that there is a tendency in many parts of this country to persecute a man now because he is a Catholic. They also know that their Church has persecuted in times past, whenever and wherever it had the power; and they know that Protestants, when in power, have always persecuted Catholics; and they know, in their hearts, that all persecution, whether in the name of law, or religion, is monstrous, savage, and fiendish.[171]

Lastly, Col. Ingersoll made a few concluding remarks that spoke to the significance of the trial and the effect of a conviction.

---

[170] Ibid., p. 78.

[171] Robert G. Ingersoll. *Trial of C.B. Reynolds for Blasphemy at Morristown, N.J., May 19th and 20th, 1887* New York City: C. P. Farrell (1888), pp. 79-80.

Any church that imprisons a man because he has used an argument against its creed, will simply convince the world that it cannot answer the argument.[172]

He also challenged the authority of the state to limit the liberty of some speech without, necessarily, limiting all speech.

If another man has not the right to think, you have not even the right to think that he thinks wrong. If every man has not the right to think, the people of New Jersey had no right to make a statute, or to adopt a Constitution – no jury has the right to render a verdict, and no court to pass its sentence.

* * *

It is impossible that there should be such a thing as real religion, without liberty. Without liberty there can be no such thing as conscience, no such word as justice. All human actions - all good, all bad – have for a foundation the idea of human liberty, and without liberty there can be no vice, and there can be no virtue.[173]

After Col. Ingersoll was again seated, Prosecutor Cutler made his closing statement to the jury.

[Prosecutor Cutler] declared: "The only question is, did the defendant circulate the pamphlet and was that pamphlet blasphemous? He did circulate it; it was blasphemous." The law is constitutional. It is in force. If the jury does its duty they should convict the defendant.[174]

The *New York Times* reporter at the trial summarized the statement to the jury by Prosecutor Cutler as follows.

Prosecutor Cutler had only a plain statement to make, and he made it clearly. He said the jury must judge by the facts and not by

---

[172] Ibid., p. 80.

[173] Ibid., p. 82. This last point is a core Christian tenet – that an individual sins through the exercise of free will. If there were no free will, no individual could reasonably be held accountable for committing a sin.

[174] "Slumbering, but Still Alive, Was Law in Famous Blasphemy Case" *Newark Evening News* January 3, 1925.

argument. If the pamphlet circulated by the defendant contained matter which came within the legal definition of blasphemy – oral or written matter casting reproach on the Christian religion or on the name or attributes of God – the verdict should be guilty. If the matter distributed was not blasphemous the defendant should go free. Believing it to be blasphemous in the meaning of the law, and believing that society must be protected by the enforcement of law, he asked for a verdict of guilty. That was all there was to the closing plea and everyone understood it.[175]

Once Prosecutor Cutler was seated, Judge Child commenced his instructions to the jury before adjourning them to the jury room to deliberate their verdict.

You will notice that the defendant is on trial for libel, and it is called a blasphemous libel, because it denies and contumeliously reproaches the holy name of God; because it contumeliously reproaches Jesus Christ and the holy word of God. Blasphemy consists in the denial of the being, attributes, or nature of, or uttering impious and profane things against, God or the authority of the holy scriptures; but it is only committed but uttering such things in a scoffing and railing manner, out of a reproachful disposition, as it were, in the speaker, rather than with any purpose of propagating his irreverent opinion. If he has merely asserted his disbelief in all the popular notions of Christianity, without attempting by impious and abusive of blasphemous remarks to wound the feelings of the whole Christian community, he will not have committed an offense of which the law can take notice. You will further observe that the defendant is not on trial for the principles of his religious belief. The laws of this state recognize no standard of faith, nor any established form of worship.
There is no offense known to our laws as heresy or nonconformity. If you are satisfied from the evidence that the defendant circulated the alleged libel, and that the same is blasphemous, and that the same was written, published, and circulated for the purpose of scoffing at, or railing and bringing into dispute the Christian religion in that respect, and out of a reproachful disposition in the writer, and calculated and intended to wound the feelings of the Christian community, then the defendant is guilty in manner and form as he stands charged. It has been said, gentlemen , that the words contained

---

[175] "Jersey Law Triumphant: Reynolds Found Guilty of Blasphemy" *New York Times* May 21, 1887, p. 8.

in this indictment are not blasphemous; that is, they are not scoffing and railing, that they are not uttered with a reproachful spirit, and that they are not calculated to wound the religious sentiment entertained by a large portion of the community. This is a question for you to judge. You can read them over. You can read them with care, as found in the indictment, and after having read them, then you are to pass that judgment on those words that you think under your oaths, and acting in the discharge of an important duty, they are entitled to. But it is said in this case that the law under which this prosecution is maintained is obsolete – that it is dead. The law on this subject is not obsolete or dead. It is to-day the living expression of the will of the people in reference to this particular matter, and you have no right to disregard or make this law a dead letter, or refuse to enforce it, than you have to repeal or abrogate any other law on the statute books protecting citizens in their rights of person or property. You, gentlemen, are not possessed, as has been well remarked, with arbitrary powers. You do not have legislative functions. It is your duty to pass on existing laws, and as you find them, not to cavil at, not to question, the wisdom or propriety of that enactment. It has been enacted by a power far above you, by a power representing the people and it is the expression of the will of the people

that comes before us here as the law, and it is a mistake that a jury or a member of a jury has a right to do as he pleases. He has not that right. He is bound as a good citizen, he is bound by the oath he has taken, he is bound by his conscience, to administer justice in this case according to the law of the land – not as he wishes it, not as he would have it, but as he finds it. He is under the law, restrained by the law, protected by the law, directed by the law, as much in the jury room as he is out of it. Now, gentlemen, what is the history of this case? And I will say here that there may be an honest difference of opinion, as there undoubtedly is an honest difference of opinion as to the propriety of this enactment. You may have your individual views. I may have my individual views. It may be that I would wish the law different than what it is. You may wish the law more stringent than we find it. So it is with every law. There is not a law on the statute books but what you will find an honest difference of opinion in reference to. As to the law in reference to capital punishment – the punishment visited for the gravest offenses committed against the law – men differ, and differ widely, but can it be held that because a juror differed as to the wisdom of that law that therefore a person arraigned before him on a charge of murder, with evidence proving his guilt beyond a reasonable doubt, that that man should be acquitted because a juror doubted the wisdom of the law? What is law? We say the law forbids this, or commands that – what do we mean by law? We have heard the learned advocate for the defendant in this case. With beautiful words, impassioned manner, and with speech so glowing as to send a thrill to every heart, he has pictured the beauties of liberty. But where is the essence of liberty – where is the evidence of it? Is it not in the great power vested in self-government? And where is the evidence of self-government save in the power to enact laws by the people for the government of all the people? And what is law, I ask you? The learned commentator says it is a rule of action prescribed by the supreme power of the state. And where do we find here the supreme power lodged? Where is sovereignty here? It reposes in the people. Then what is law? It is a rule prescribed by the people for the government of the people. It is not the will of the legislature, not the say-so of a body of men who are in power to-day and away to-morrow – that is not law. And so, when we say that there is on the statute books of the state of New Jersey a law that says, 'No man shall commit blasphemy,' that is the same as saying that the power of the people exercising the sovereignty reposed in them has declared that thus is the will of the people of the state of New Jersey. What secures freedom of speech? What guarantees to a defendant the right to trial by jury? What gives the processes of court to compel the attendance of witnesses? What is it that prevents the courts from closing the mouth of his counsel? It is the law. And how long, gentlemen – think of it – could freedom of speech exist without law? Now, gentlemen, does this law interfere with the freedom of speech? On that question I have an opinion delivered by probably one of the most eminent students of the Constitution that this country ever saw – a gentleman whose writings are found in every library, whose opinions are quoted almost as gospel; and he, passing on a case exactly similar to this, says: 'The free and equal and undisturbed enjoyment of religious opinion, whatever it may be, and free and decent discussion on any religious subject is guaranteed and secured; but to revile with malicious and blasphemous contempt the religion professed by almost the whole community is an abuse of this right.' And in that same case this law under discussion – and so I charge you – was held to be perfectly constitutional, and that it was no invasion of the rights of the citizen so far as freedom of speech was concerned. Now, gentlemen, it is said that this is an obsolete law. This law is found first, so far as we are concerned, back in the colonial days of this state. Almost at the first formation of the state government it was enacted as a law. In 1844 the law was again adopted by the people as the rule of conduct with reference to this particular subject matter. In 1874, - not fourteen years ago – only a little over thirteen years ago – the people of the state of New Jersey represented in the legislature by their representatives, enacted this same law again as the rule of conduct that they prescribed for the government of all the people of this state. There it is. And, gentlemen, I desire to call your attention again to this fact, that your duty as jurors is limited solely to passing upon the question of the existence of the law and the question of the violation of the law. With the wisdom of the enactment you have nothing to do. That power is vested in the people and exercised by them through the legislature. Since this very bill was formed, since this indictment was presented, the people of this state have assembled through their representatives at the state capital. The doors were open. This case had notoriety. If it was the desire and wish of the people that this law should be stricken from the statute book, there was the proper tribunal to appeal to, and power vested with ample jurisdiction over this matter. But it is enough for us to know that it is the law, and being the law, we are bound to enforce it; and if this defendant has been proved to your satisfaction, beyond the reasonable doubt I have referred to, to have committed the crime of blasphemy, it is your duty to convict him. If he has not, it is your duty to acquit him. Let him be acquitted, or let him be convicted, because he has either violated, or not violated, the law. Do not acquit him by violating the law yourself.[176]

The *New York Times* reporter at the trial summarized Judge Child's instructions to the jury as follows:

There was no nonsense about the manner in which [Judge Child] set out to do up Col. Ingersoll, an effort in which the presence of the representative people of the place was by no means a dispiriting influence. He cautioned the jury with much emphasis that they had nothing to do with the wisdom of the Grand Jury in finding an indictment, or with the motives of the witnesses before the Grand Jury, or with the law as measure of sense. The law was in the statutes, and the only question was had it been violated by the person on trial. If the offense had been proved against him beyond a reasonable doubt, he was guilty. Heresy and nonconformity were not known to the law of the State. A man might hold what opinions he chose, but if he uttered profane things against God or the Christian religion in a scoffing or railing manner, calculated to wound the sentiment of the community, he was guilty of blasphemy under the law. The law was not dead or obsolete. From the fact that it stood on the statutes it was to be presumed that it expressed the will of the

---

[176] "Convicted and Fined" *The Truth Seeker* Vol. 14, No. 22, May 28, 1887, pp. 344-345. Judge Child sums up by nearly threatening the jury that they would be violating the law if they acquitted Reynolds on the basis of free speech protections in the U. S. Constitution.

people. A jury had no more right to repel it or set it aside than to set aside any law involving life or property. No jury could do as it pleased. It had to take the law as it found it, not as it would have it. Through all history there had been honest differences of opinion in regard to laws. Men differed widely on the subject of capital punishment. Yet a jury would not be justified anywhere in failing to bring in a verdict of guilty in a murder case solely on the ground that a man would have to suffer death. Judge Child went on to put more spikes in the great pleader's guns. It was a beautiful speech, he said, that the jury had heard, splendid in sentiment, and expressed with a vigor to thrill every heart. But wherein, the court urged, with the warmth of an advocate, law the essence of liberty in law? Law was a rule prescribed by the people for the government of the people. When a law on the statutes said that such no man should commit blasphemy, that law meant that such was the will of the people. In a case similar to this in another State the law had been held to be perfectly constitutional, and no invasion of rights so far as freedom of speech was concerned.
Reverting to Col. Ingersoll's assertion that the law was obsolete, Judge Child said that although it was true that it originated in colonial days, it had been re-enacted in 1844 and it was allowed to stand as the will of the people upon the revision of the laws in 1874. Indeed, since this indictment the Legislature had met and no one had thought it worthwhile even to suggest a change in the law. "Therefore," said Judge Child, "let the defendant be convicted or acquitted. He violated the law or he did not. Do not acquit him by violating the law yourselves."[177]

According to *The Truth Seeker*, Judge Child appeared to demand a guilty verdict by the jury.

It was evident after the first five minutes that the district-attorney and judge had 'swapped jobs.' Mr. Cutler had been cool and comparatively mild. The judge was the opposite. His words were not a judicial charge to a jury, but a heated and very slightly disguised appeal for conviction. He raised his voice in temper, pounded the bench to emphasize his points, and throughout his speech was the advocate for his religion and the prosecutor of him who had brought it into contempt. His zeal betrayed him. Legally expressed, the case at this point was Colonel Ingersoll for the

[177] "Jersey Law Triumphant: Reynolds Found Guilty of Blasphemy" *New York Times* May 21, 1887, p. 8.

defendant, Judge Child for the plaintiff; and the plaintiff's attorney made it a matter of personal pride to win. It was not often he got the chance to argue against so distinguished a man as Colonel Ingersoll, and the opportunity must be made the most of.[178]

Judge Child charged the jury at 10:45 a.m. At about 12:00 noon, the jury sent word that they had reached a verdict. The court was reconvened, and at 12:15 p.m., jury foreman Jacob Ogden informed the court clerk that the verdict was "Guilty." Judge Child then dismissed the jury.[179]

Prosecutor Cutler could not be quickly located so Judge Child recessed the court for dinner and reconvened at 1:00 p.m. Judge Child sentenced Reynolds.

[Judge Child] said sternly, "Charles B. Reynolds, stand up." Mr. Reynolds stood up. "You have been convicted," continued Mr. Child, "of circulating blasphemous matter. Inasmuch as the law has for so long been unused, you may reasonably be expected to have been ignorant of it. And while ignorance of the law excuses no man from its penalties, the court feels bound to take the fact of your ignorance into consideration in passing sentence. The judgment of the court is that you pay a fine of twenty-five dollars, together with the costs of prosecution, and stand committed till paid."[180]

Colonel Ingersoll stated that he was prepared to pay the fine and court costs. The Clerk of the Court estimated these costs at $75 and Colonel Ingersoll wrote out a check[181].

---

178 "Convicted and Fined" *The Truth Seeker* Vol. 14, No. 22, May 28, 1887, p. 344.
179 Ibid., p. 345.
180 Ibid., p. 345.
181 The editor of *The Truth Seeker* eventually obtained a detailed bill of costs for the blasphemy trial from Melvin S. Condit, the Clerk of the Court. The total costs were $68.21. See "The Costs in Reynolds's Trial for Blasphemy" *The Truth Seeker*, Vol. 14, No. 38, September 17, 1887, p. 595.

Prosecutor Cutler advised Judge Child that he would not prosecute the indictment for blasphemy in Boonton. *The Truth Seeker* commented that this action and the light fine were influenced by other factors as well.

This back-down was not altogether unexpected. When the verdict was rendered, Colonel Ingersoll at once moved for a new trial, but during the hunt for the prosecutor it was found that the two lay judges, Messrs. Quimby and Munson, were opposed to the punishment of heresy, and insisted upon a light fine as the penalty on the conviction secured, and a dismissal of the other indictment. The prosecutor was also willing that the matter be disposed of in that way. With the exception of Child, the court felt, as a daily paper put it, willing to let up on Mr. Reynolds if Colonel Ingersoll would let up on the court. After his speech on Thursday, the Baptist and Methodist preachers of the place approached Colonel Ingersoll and told him they agreed with "every word he had said." A young lawyer, the son of the Presbyterian parson of the place, said the same. Though the ministers doubtless exaggerated their agreement, there was no doubt that the speech had a great influence upon public sentiment. The judges knew of this, and when Colonel Ingersoll told them that if they tried Mr. Reynolds upon the other indictment, he would come down and convert the whole town, they thought the joke might have a serious side.[182]

The *New York Times* summed up the decision not to prosecute the second indictment as follows:

A little confab led [Prosecutor Cutler] to say that he would not press the untried indictment for blasphemy at Boonton. The records were then fixed up to suit the state of affairs, and the great Reynolds case had passed into history.[183]

The *Boston Investigator* explained the decision of Col. Ingersoll not to pursue a retrial or appeal as follows:

---

182 "Convicted and Fined" *The Truth Seeker* Vol. 14, No. 22, May 28, 1887, p. 345.

183 "Jersey Law Triumphant: Reynolds Found Guilty of Blasphemy" *New York Times* May 21, 1887, p. 8.

The jury, after being out an hour, announced a verdict of guilty. After the Judge's charge, no one was surprised at this. Col. Ingersoll at first moved for a new trial, but action being postponed in the temporary absence of the prosecutor, he subsequently thought better of it when he found that the Court and the prosecutor were anxious to drop the matter as expeditiously as they might. An understanding was therefore reached by which the Court was to let up on the prisoner, and the Colonel was to let up on the Court..."Why didn't you take the case to a higher court?" Col. Ingersoll was asked.
"Oh! It would be too much bother," he replied impatiently. "We couldn't gain anything more than we have already. They virtually abandoned the whole thing as soon as they got a verdict with which to let themselves down easy."[184]

In the aftermath of the trial, the reporter for the *New York Times* spoke to jurors and learned that there were two ballots in the jury room. The juror Benjamin Flaherty, a miner and a Catholic, voted for acquittal on the first ballot but voted with the majority on the second ballot.[185]

Following the trial, on May 28, 1887, Reynolds commented on his conviction in a column that appeared in *The Truth Seeker*.

To attempt to correct or contradict the many silly and malicious misrepresentations in some secular and many religious papers would be useless. But I do desire that all Liberals should know the facts. Even according to the Jersey law I was not guilty of blasphemy. There is no low, improper, or obscene word in my pamphlet, "Blasphemy and the Bible," for the free distribution of which I was indicted. The pamphlet was written in self-defense, simply for the desire to prove that the Bible and those who insist that its every word is inspired of God were the real blasphemers; that the Bible was not a safe moral guide; nor the best saints of the Old Testament, indorsed

---

184 "Trial and Conviction of C. B. Reynolds for Blasphemy" *Boston Investigator* May 25, 1887, Issue 7, p. 3.
185 Ibid., p. 8.

by the New, persons whose example it was safe or creditable to follow.[186]

The Rev. Hugh O. Pentecost commented on the trial and his words probably best express the popular sentiment.

...Will men never learn anything from history? It seems incredible that a statute against blasphemy can be operative in this or any state. This silly and wicked statute has succeeded in giving a thousand times the circulation to Mr. Reynolds's pamphlet that it otherwise would have had. I am a Christian minister, but in my opinion if God and the Christian religion cannot take care of themselves without a resort to courts of human law, both are in a bad way. Truth can take care of itself. If we have the truth we need not fear blasphemers. If Reynolds has the truth, judges and jurors will not suppress it. That cause is a very weak one which will not bear discussion. I venture the opinion that there are many Christians in New Jersey who are ashamed of the Reynolds trial and conviction, as I certainly am....[187]

---

[186] "A Letter from Mr. Reynolds" *The Truth Seeker*, Vol. 14, No. 23, June 4, 1887, p. 357

[187] George E. MacDonald. *Fifty Years of Freethought* 2 vols. New York: Arno Press & The New York Times (1972) [reprint of 1929 ed.], pp. 422-423. The following year, in 1888, the Rev. Hugh O. Pentecost revealed that he had become an agnostic (p. 465).

Later Years

Reynolds continued his lectures for the American Secular Union after his conviction for blasphemy in New Jersey. He commenced a series of lecturing tours in the West almost immediately. During 1888, Reynolds traveled widely including Albuquerque, New Mexico (March), San Diego, California (April), San Jose, California (May), Marshfield, Oregon (August), Pasco, Washington Territory (September) and Nebraska and Dakota (December). The lecturing tour continued into 1989 including Minnesota, Illinois, Michigan and finally concluded at Reynolds' home in North Parma, New York. In all, the 1888-1889 lecturing tour of the West was very difficult and Reynolds was ill with "inflammatory rheumatism" for more than three weeks after he arrived home.[188]

"I have been away from home 18 months, and during that time, have not missed over 25 nights that I did not lecture."[189]

After Reynolds recovered his health, he and his wife decided to relocate from New York to Washington Territory. On the way there, they attended the annual convention of the American Secular Union in Cleveland, Ohio.

Mrs. Reynolds is advertised to lecture before the Secular Union, at Cleveland, Ohio, Sunday, April 14th. I shall accompany her there, as we have decided to go to Walla Walla, Wash. Ter., and make that place our headquarters for the next three months, with a view of

---

[188] C. B. Reynolds. "The Tent Once More in the Field" *Boston Investigator* April 10, 1889, Issue 1, p. 6.

[189] C. B. Reynolds. "C. B. Reynolds on His Western Tour" *Boston Investigator* March 6, 1889, Issue 48, p. 3.

making our permanent home in that, or some other, city of Washington Ter. or Oregon.[190]

Reynolds stayed for a while in Walla Walla, Washington Territory. He lectured on Sunday evenings at Small's Opera House for eight months in 1889 at the invitation of the Liberal Club.[191] Reynolds and his wife lectured throughout Oregon and Washington.

During November 1889, Reynolds visited Seattle and he commented on the destruction of the downtown business district caused by the great fire.

On the 6th of June last, the fire fiend in a few hours destroyed buildings and property to the amount of twenty million dollars, on which the total insurance was less than three millions. The burnt district included forty blocks or over eighty acres, exclusive of the water front, comprising eighteen blocks, making the total devastation 116 acres. In this vast area not a single building escaped destruction. The loss however was confined entirely to the business portion of the city.[192]

On the same trip, Reynolds visited Port Townsend, Washington Territory and he marveled at how busy it was.

Port Townsend is situated at the head of the Straits of Juan de Fuca, and commands the entrance to the whole [Puget] Sound country. It is one of the finest harbors in the known world. Port Townsend bay has an anchorage area of about 50 square miles, more tonnage is registered at Port Townsend than any other port in the entire United States. The official report of the business transacted at the Customs

---

190 C. B. Reynolds. "The Tent Once More in the Field" *Boston Investigator* April 10, 1889, Issue 1, p. 6.

191 Samuel P. Putnam. *400 Years of Freethought* New York: *The Truth Seeker Company* (1894), pp. 793-794. Washington was admitted to statehood on November 11, 1889.

192 C. B. Reynolds. "Ex-Rev. C. B. Reynolds' Tour of Washington" *Boston Investigator* Dec. 4, 1889, Issue 35, p. 3.

House from Dec. '87, to Nov. '88, gives the number of vessels cleared 1046, total tonnage 966,356. Number of vessels entered Dec. '87, to Nov. '88, 1039, total tonnage 1,049,004. The report for '89 will greatly exceed this.[193]

Another traveling lecturer, and the secretary of the American Secular Union, Samuel P. Putnam, had lectured throughout the Washington Territory during 1887 and helped organize the Seattle Secular Union.[194] Reynolds helped organize the Washington Secular Union and served as secretary. The Washington Secular Union held its first state convention in Seattle during January 28-30, 1890.[195]

...when in 1890 the Washington Secular Union held its first convention, the speakers' end of the hall was hung with a mammoth oil painting that reproduced a Truth Seeker cartoon of 'Uncle Sam and His Parasites,' over which a red, white and blue banner proclaimed "Keep Church and State Forever Separate." To the right was a banner: 'Infidelity is Liberty – All Religion is Slavery.' To the left, above a portrait of Paine: 'To do Good is My Religion.'[196]

---

[193] C. B. Reynolds. "Ex.-Rev. C. B. Reynolds' Tour in Washington" *Boston Investigator* Dec. 11, 1889, Issue 36, p. 2.

[194] "News and Notes" *The Truth Seeker*, Vol. 14, No. 30, August 13, 1887, p. 516. There is no mention of the Seattle Secular Union in any newspapers – including freethought publications - and it is likely that its members became part of the Washington Secular Union.

[195] C. B. Reynolds. "Practical Work in Washington: The Taxed and the Untaxed" *Boston Investigator* January 22, 1890, Issue 42, p. 2.

[196] Philip Hamburger. *Separation of Church and State* Cambridge, MA: Harvard University Press (2002), p. 320.

Hamburger cites the "Washington Secular Union" *Freethought: A Liberal Journal*, 3 (no. 8): 121 (Feb. 22, 1890). There are no records about this convention in the Seattle newspapers, Seattle Public Library, University of Washington library, Seattle Genealogical Society library or other local collections. An article by Charles Reynolds that appeared in the *Boston Investigator* offers an insight into the reason for the absence of any records:

C. B. Reynolds. "The Cause in Washington" *Boston Investigator* May 4, 1892, Issue 5, p. 3. "At the organization of our state union no newspaper in this city [Seattle] would give us one line of notice –

The office of the Washington Secular Union was originally established at 2104 Sixth Street in Seattle. Reynolds moved to Fremont, then a suburb of Seattle, to keep his living expenses low. He traveled from Fremont to the post office in Seattle by electric street car. The street cars made the trip every 20 minutes and the trip took 15 minutes. The fare was five cents.[197]

According to entries in city directories, and the 1892 Census, Reynolds lived on Kilbourne Avenue in Ward 9 of Seattle during 1892.[198] Next, he resided in Tacoma at 912 S. 15th during 1893-1895.[199]

In May, 1892, [Reynolds] accepted an engagement as lecturer for the Tacoma Secular Union, and from that date has lectured every Sunday evening at Germania Hall, Tacoma, the largest hall in the city. On

---

even for pay." According to Reynolds, there was a similar situation in the nearby city of Tacoma:
C. B. Reynolds. "The Tacoma Secular Union" *Boston Investigator* Dec. 28, 1892, Issue 39, p. 3. "The Tacoma Secular Union, of Tacoma, Wash., continues its career of usefulness and uninterrupted prosperity. For seven months we have lectures every Sunday, at the Germania Hall (the largest and most popular hall in the city), and despite the fierce opposition of the ministerial alliance collectively, and the malice, misrepresentations and desperate endeavors of the clergy and Christian bigots individually, without a single line of notice in any of the daily papers (stopped under threat of withdrawal of Christian advertising), the interest is maintained, and our attendance, consisting of the most intelligent and many of the most influential people of the city, exceeds that of any three of the churches."

197 C. B. Reynolds. "Washington Secular Union" *Boston Investigator* January 21, 1891, Issue 42, p. 3.

198 *Census of the Inhabitants in the 9th Ward, Seattle, County of King, State of Washington* (1892), line 16, roll V228_7.

199 R. L. Polk & Co's. *Tacoma City Directory. 1893-1894*, p. 665; 1895, p. 520.

Sunday, Aug. 6, 1893, he inaugurated the Tacoma Secular Sunday-school, which has proved a great success.[200]

The offices of the Washington Secular Union were moved from Seattle to 420 N. L Street in Tacoma when Reynolds relocated to be nearer to his lecturing engagements.

The second convention of the Washington Secular Union was held at the G.A.R. Hall, Second Street, in Seattle on Sunday, February 22, 1891. This convention authorized the purchase of a type-writer for the Secretary (Reynolds) at an estimated cost of $100. The convention also reappointed Reynolds as the Secretary of the W.S.U. and appointed Mrs. F. C. Reynolds as Field Secretary of the W.S.U. Her duties were to lecture and assist liberals in establishing local unions.[201]

The Washington Secular Union was very active in opposing paid chaplain positions in the state legislature in an effort to keep separate church and state. The W.S.U. also opposed religious activities in public schools. Perhaps their greatest success was in opposing Sunday laws that were promoted by clergy from mainstream religious sects.

To the pretence that Christians are disturbed and cannot enjoy their religious worship on Sunday because some are quietly following business or amusement, we [W.S.U.] call attention that Jews, Seventh-Day Adventists and Seventh Day Baptists always worship

---

[200] Samuel P. Putnam. *400 Years of Freethought* New York: *The Truth Seeker Company* (1894), pp. 794. See also, George E. MacDonald. *Fifty Years of Freethought* 2 vols. New York: Arno Press & The New York Times (1972) [reprint of 1929 ed.], Vol. 2, pp. 130-131. MacDonald adds: "Afterward, till the time of his death, he was speaker for the Secular Church of Portland, Oregon."
[201] C. B. Reynolds. "Washington Secular Union" *Boston Investigator* March 25, 1891, Issue 51, p. 3.

on Saturday – the only true Sabbath of God, Christ, and the Bible; the very busiest day of all the week, yet they find no difficulty in enjoying their work.[202]

By 1896, Reynolds again lived in Seattle on Bowman Avenue in the Fremont neighborhood. Reynolds was visiting McMinnville, Oregon to make a funeral address when he fell from a swing and struck his head. Reynolds returned to Seattle and a few days later, on July 31, 1896, he died.[203]

The causes which brought about the death of Mr. Reynolds were peculiar. He was down in Oregon ten days ago. One evening as he was sitting in a swing he accidentally fell out backwards, striking on his head. The following day he was able to deliver a funeral oration over the remains of an old time friend, but he never got over the result of the blow. He returned to his Fremont home feeling poorly and his death last evening was the direct result of the blow on his head.[204]

Reynolds was buried at Mt. Pleasant Cemetery in Seattle on August 2, 1896, a few days after George Grow, the father-in-law of his youngest child Gertrude Reynolds. Long-time editor of *The Truth Seeker* and personal friend, George E. MacDonald, summed up Reynolds's qualities in his book *Fifty Years of Freethought.*

---

[202] C. B. Reynolds. "Victory of Washington Secular Union" *Boston Investigator* December 17, 1890, Issue 37, p. 3.
[203] The Death Certificate shows his date of death as July 31, 1896 and his cause of death as meningitis.
[204] "Fell from a Swing: C. B. Reynolds Died at Fremont Last Evening from Injuries" *The Seattle Times*, Saturday, August 1, 1896, p. 8. See also, George E. MacDonald. *Fifty Years of Freethought* 2 vols. New York: Arno Press & The New York Times (1972) [reprint of 1929 ed.], Vol. 2, pp. 130-131. "His death was caused by a fall from a swing in which he was sitting while in McMinnwille, Oregon, whither he had been called to deliver the funeral address of an old-time Liberal. Concussion of the brain resulted fatally about a week after he reached his home"

Reynolds was a man of character and courage and culture, with an uncanny knowledge of scriptural texts and ability to locate them; an always ready speaker, a good friend and companion, an honest, worthy, and sincere Freethinker.[205]

[205] George E. MacDonald. *Fifty Years of Freethought* 2 vols. New York: Arno Press & The New York Times (1972) [reprint of 1929 ed.], Vol. 2, pp. 130-131.

Significance of Trial

As is generally true with historical events, it is difficult to estimate the true significance of the Reynolds blasphemy trial without a full understanding of the times.

The nineteenth century was characterized by numerous events of enormous import. It was an age of science, invention and expansion. And, of course, the Civil War.

> From the perspective of changes to the landscape of American society, the century from 1790 to 1890 was dominated by three phenomena: (1) Manifest Destiny and the frontier; (2) slavery, states rights, and the Civil War; and (3) cultural diversification largely brought about by the 'great immigration.' [206]

The institutions and traditions of colonial times had undergone profound change. The industrial revolution had transformed the nation from a farm to a factory economy and the population had shifted from rural to urban as a result. Waves of immigrants from Europe changed the character of the large cities and helped to settle the West.

> By 1890, one in four Americans had foreign-born parents and almost one in five (the highest level ever recorded by the Census Bureau) was foreign born. [207]

All of these changes unsettled religious practices and beliefs that had persisted for centuries. The first half of the nineteenth century saw a proliferation of Protestant sects. For instance, various millennial groups evolved

---

[206] William M. Newman and Peter L. Halvorson. *Atlas of American Religion: The Denominational Era 1776-1990* Walnut Creek, CA: Alta Mira Press (2000), p. 26.
[207] Ibid., p. 30

into new sects including Jehovah's Witnesses and the Seventh-day Adventists. Other indigenous sects formed as well including the Church of Jesus Christ of the Latter Day Saints (the Mormons) and Christian Scientists. The divisiveness of the slavery issue and the Civil War led to schism and the creation of new sects, most notably the Southern Methodists and Southern Baptists. Finally, the great numbers of immigrants from Ireland, Italy and Eastern Europe added large Catholic communities in many northeast cities which had previously been overwhelmingly Protestant.

Even as the percentage of church adherents was growing from an estimated 10% of the 4 million population in 1790 to 26% of the 23 million population in 1850 and 45% of the 63 million population in 1890, there was rapid growth of a liberal or secular movement. The secular movement membership was primarily non-adherents of religious organizations.[208]

The long Civil War and the unprecedented devastation it wrought, as well as the conflicted morality of the slavery issue, led to disillusionment with religion on the part of many. The famous attorney Col. Robert G. Ingersoll, a prolific writer and lecturer, spoke about this frequently. The growth of the secular movement and the challenges to religious doctrine posed by scientific discoveries such as Darwin's theory of natural selection (evolution) combined to prompt the emergence of new, fundamentalist religious sects. By the end of the century, the conflict between science and religion largely collapsed when mainstream religious sects abandoned a strictly literal interpretation of biblical scripture for a more allegorical understanding.

---

[208] Ibid., pp. 27, 33.

Why did strong secularism fail to achieve its professed twin goals of freeing the American mind from the baleful influence of religion and reordering the relationship between government and religion in America? Part of the answer is that mainline American religion rose to the challenge that science posed to traditional faith by offering a reconciliation of the two. By allowing for an allegorical reinterpretation of Scripture that was consistent with the pervasive influence of science and technology, liberal Christianity made it unnecessary for college students exposed to Darwinism or psychology to abandon their belief in God. For organized religion to survive in America, God-centered theology had to take a back seat to pragmatic, community-centered concerns – and it was prepared to do so, giving way to a social gospel that focused on human concerns and minimized the role of theology.[209]

Church acceptance of Darwin's theory of natural selection was made possible by retaining divine creation as the First Cause and source of all natural laws that fashioned the world as we find it.

...The Biblical view of Creation was reconciled with the evolutionary concept of origination by interpreting the former as an orderly and progressive scheme of development from lower to higher forms of life and intelligence, and from inferior to superior conditions of existence. Evolution, most pulpits now argued, simply furnished a more orderly and progressive series of effects; it did not dispense with the first Great Cause.[210]

This conclusion found strong support from eminent writers on the history of science such as Bertrand Russell.

The conflict between theology and science was quite as much a conflict between authority and observation. The men of science did not ask that propositions should be believed because some important authority had said they were true; quite the contrary, they appealed to the evidence of the senses, and maintained only such doctrines as

---

[209] Noah Feldman. *Divided by God: America's Church-State Problem* New York: Farrar, Straus and Giroux (2005), pp. 147-148.
[210] Sidney Warren. *American Freethought 1860-1914* New York: Gordian Press Inc. (1966) [orig. published 1943], p. 69.

they believed to be based upon facts which were patent to all who chose to make the necessary observations. The new method achieved such immense successes, both theoretical and practical, that theology was gradually forced to accommodate itself to science. Inconvenient Bible texts were interpreted allegorically or figuratively; Protestants transferred the seat of authority in religion, first from the Church and the Bible alone, and then to the individual soul. It came gradually to be recognized that the religious life does not depend on pronouncements as to matters of fact, for instance, the historical existence of Adam and Eve. Thus religion, by surrendering the outworks, has sought to preserve the citadel intact – whether successfully or not remains to be seen.[211]

Initially, the secular movement was dominated by deists who thrived during the Age of Enlightenment in the previous century and inherited the philosophy of Epicurus.

Deism in British North America played a major role in the development of the views that gave rise to the American Revolution and to the content of the U.S. Constitution. The deist's belief in human rationality, human improvement (if not perfectability), and universal moral standards (including natural law and natural rights) that were applicable to all people at all times deeply influenced American views of constitutional government and of religious tolerance and liberty. The influence of these deistic views is obvious in the language of the Declaration of Independence (of its 56 signers, 52 were deists). Deists also predominated in the Continental Congress and among the generals in the Continental Army.[212]

Ultimately, the rapid growth of modern science in the aftermath of major scientific discoveries generally undermined long held religious doctrines based upon the literal truth of the Scriptures.

---

[211] Bertrand Russell. *Religion and Science* New York: Oxford University Press (1935), pp. 16-17.

[212] Edward L. Queen II, Stephen R. Prothero, and Gardiner H. Shattuck Jr. *Encyclopedia of American Religious History* 3rd ed., Vol. I "A-E", p. 29.

American secularism, as it eventually emerged in the 1870s and '80s, was not Holyoake's movement [Great Britain] but rather a gradually growing development in educated circles embracing rationalism and science over traditional religious belief. The true aim of this strong secularism was the full replacement of religion by reason, both in the realm of belief and in the political sphere.[213]

The secular movement of the late nineteenth century found considerable support in two noteworthy books by academics that sought to explain the conflict between science and religion.

Two books written in the 1870s and widely read for decades laid the scientific groundwork for American strong secularism as not just an intellectual position but an ideology: Andrew Dickson White's work, *The Warfare of Science* (1876)...and *The History of the Conflict Between Religion and Science* by New York University chemist – turned-historian John William Draper, published in 1876. Although neither of these books used the word "secularism," both were serious, systematic efforts by members in good-standing of the educational elite to promote reason to the detriment of doctrinal religious faith.[214]

The authors of these books did not agree entirely. Prof. Andrew Dickson White, in his *A History of the Warfare of Science with Theology in Christendom*, distinguished between his conclusions and those of Prof. John W. Draper as follows:

...(M)uch as I admired Draper's treatment of the questions involved, his point of view and mode of looking at history were different from mine. (Draper) regarded the struggle as one between Science and Religion. I believed then, and am convinced now, that it was a struggle between Science and Dogmatic Theology. More and more I

---

[213] Noah Feldman. *Divided by God: America's Church State Problem* New York: Farrar, Straus and Giroux (2005), p. 114. Holyoake was the leader of the secular movement in Great Britain. Secularism in Great Britain represented a working class revolt against religion that was seen as a tool of their oppressors.

[214] Ibid., p. 115.

saw that it was the conflict between two epochs in the evolution of human thought – the theological and the scientific.[215]

Many modern historians and Christian apologists believe, as White did, that there is no necessary conflict between science and religion because they deal with different worlds – the physical and spiritual. However, that perspective ignores the many instances where there is no clear separation between church and state including abortion rights, teaching evolution in public schools, physician-assisted suicide, the death penalty, school prayer, stem cell research, and homosexual marriage just to name a few. The conflict remains especially real among fundamentalist sects who promote the literal truth of the Scriptures lest the entire word of God be doubted and subject to reinterpretation.

It was this literalist, dogmatic religion that John William Draper was speaking of when he stated that,

Faith is in its nature unchangeable, stationary; science is in its nature progressive; and eventually a divergence between them, impossible to conceal, must take place.[216]

Draper summarized the impact of new scientific discoveries on modern society by stating that, "Intellectually, (science) overthrew the authority of tradition…"; "It refused to accept, unless accompanied by proof, the dicta of any master, no matter how eminent…"; and "It rejected the supernatural and miraculous as evidence…" According to Draper,

[215] Andrew Dickson White. *A History of the Warfare of Science with Theology in Christendom* 2 vols. New York: D. Appleton and Co. (1917). p. ix.
[216] John William Draper. *History of the Conflict Between Religion and Science* New York: D. Appleton and Co. (1875), p. vii.

The history of Science is not a mere record of isolated discoveries; it is a narrative of the conflict of two contending powers, the expansive force of the human intellect on one side, and the compression arising from traditionary faith and human interests on the other.[217]

Draper argued that mathematics was the language of reason and it was replacing dogmatic belief.

The habit of mental exactness (that mathematics) encouraged extended to other branches of thought, and produced an intellectual revolution. No longer was it possible to be satisfied with miracle-proof, or the logic that had been relied upon throughout the middle ages. Not only did it thus influence the manner of thinking, it also changed the direction of thought...But the use of mathematics was not limited to the verification of theories...it also furnished a means of predicting what had hitherto been unobserved. In this it offered a counterpart to the prophecies of ecclesiasticism.[218]

He condemned religious dogmatic beliefs for retarding the intellectual development of mankind. Conversely, he asserted that science would improve mankind's circumstances.

Though not without a bitter resistance on the part of the clergy, men began to think that pestilences are not punishments inflicted by God on society for its religious shortcomings, but the physical consequences of filth and wretchedness; that the proper mode of avoiding them is not by praying to the saints, but by insuring personal and municipal cleanliness.[219]

The nineteenth century was a period of rapid and dramatic change that affected nearly every aspect of daily life. These turbulent times were, in large part, due to notable advances in all the sciences.

The year 1859 saw the publication of the most important scientific work since Isaac Newton's *Principia* of 1687: Charles Darwin's *The*

---

[217] Ibid., p. 301.
[218] Ibid., pp. 303-304.
[219] Ibid., p. 314.

Origin of Species, which not only elevated biology into the realm of theoretical science previously reserved for physics and chemistry, but immediately cast grave doubt on the biblical account of creation of life. Its sequel *The Descent of Man*, published in 1871, further undercut the religious view that man was specially created as the pinnacle and purpose of the universe. These two books appeared just as industrialization and the spread of the railroads were transforming ordinary life. Technologies such as the telegraph, the steam engine, and eventually electric power, vastly enhanced the prestige of science. Though we now take such progress for granted, each major scientific breakthrough in the modern age has challenged religious verities and led to new debates about whether traditional religion should finally be jettisoned...The remarkable successes of science and technology unsettled old religious truths and propelled a new movement toward religious skepticism and even materialism.[220]

The secular movement was a byproduct of this change.

The scientific discoveries of (the nineteenth) century resulted in an almost revolutionary transformation of men's thinking. New discoveries in physics provided a naturalistic explanation of many hitherto mysterious processes of nature; biological evolution proved that all forms of organic life, including man, had developed from simple and rudimentary types, thereby shattering the fundamentalist conception of creation; and higher biblical criticism challenged the prevailing scriptural interpretation. ...The impact of the new science generated a skepticism that infiltrated all fields of intellectual endeavor. Scientific inquiry displaced conformity, and doubt supplanted unquestioning orthodoxy. People did not, however, become indifferent to basic religious faith. Their thinking merely became more secular.[221]

The secular movement in America had its roots in the Age of Enlightenment which gradually transformed European society and intellectual life from the middle ages to the modern era. The Age of Enlightenment itself was the direct result of the birth of the modern sciences

---

220 Noah Feldman. *Divided by God: America's Church-State Problem* New York: Farrar, Straus and Giroux (2005), pp. 111-112.
221 Sidney Warren. *American Freethought, 1860-1914* New York: Gordian Press Inc. (1966) [orig. published 1943], pp. 228-229.

followed closely by technology innovations that led to the industrial revolution. Secularism, also known as freethought, was a reaction against limitations on speech imposed by the clergy and based upon religious doctrine.

In America, the founder of the secular movement was considered by many to be Thomas Paine. Paine, propagandist of the American Revolution, was enormously effective in rallying public sentiment behind the fight for independence by demanding that government be freed from tyranny. Later in life, Paine demanded freedom from religious tyranny.

> Ever since the publication in 1794 of *The Age of Reason*, Thomas Paine enjoyed the unrivalled position of patron saint of the freethought movement. If the Christian movement had its Christ, the Jewish religion had its Moses, and the Mohammedan religion its Mohammed, then the "religion" of unbelief in America, too, had its prophet. The feeling of reverence which Paine was regarded by freethinkers contrasted sharply with the scorn in which he was held by most Christian believers. This antagonism was chiefly due to the publication of *The Age of Reason* which subsequently became the bible of the freethought movement ... Where Voltaire had scarred the church with his rapier of wit, Paine "seized the bludgeon of common sense and delivered a series of shattering blows on the skull of theology."[222]

Ironically, the secular movement in America received its greatest support from the mainstream Protestant sects. Their normally divergent interests combined in favor of the separation of church and state when heavy Catholic immigration from Europe threatened the Protestant character of public life.

> Although American Protestants had long felt a profound animus against the Catholic Church, they gave this antagonism new intensity in the nineteenth century. They had inherited some very traditional fears about the anti-Christian character of Catholicism and its union

[222] Ibid., p. 110.

of church and state. In addition, they now combined these with more modern, theologically liberal anxieties about Catholic ecclesiastical authority and its threat to individual mental freedom. Viewing themselves as intellectually independent individuals, who followed their consciences rather than the authority of any church or priest, many Protestants assumed that the Catholic Church, because of its apparent threat to intellectual independence, was all the more likely to obtain political power and revive a medieval intolerance. In response to this combination of liberal and more traditional fears, Protestants would eventually elevate separation of church and state as an American ideal.[223]

The initial conflict between Protestants and Catholics that raised the church-state debate occurred in 1840 and involved public school funding in New York.[224]

The National Liberal League was established by freethinkers meeting in Philadelphia in 1876 on the centennial of the nation. Their goal was to promote separation between church and state. Freethinkers took the name "liberals" although the clergy considered them infidels. The National Liberal League changed its name to the American Secular Union in 1883.[225] This organization had chapters in many cities and towns growing from 18 branches in 1876 to 225 in 1881.[226] The American Secular Union was closely allied with various freethought publications such as *The Boston Investigator*, *The Index* and *The Truth Seeker*.

---

[223] Philip Hamburger. *Separation of Church and State* Cambridge, MA: Harvard University Press (2002), pp. 201-202.

[224] Ibid., pp. 219-220.

[225] Marshall G. Brown and Gordon Stein. *Freethought in the United States: A Descriptive Bibliography* Westport, CT: Greenwood Press (1978), p. 53.

[226] Samuel Putnam. *Four Hundred Years of Freethought*, pp. 528-532 cited by Sidney Warren *American Freethought 1860-1914* New York: Gordian Press Inc. (1966) [orig. published 1943], p. 30 Note 24.

After the Civil War, Col. Robert G. Ingersoll, a great admirer of Thomas Paine's writings, succeeded him as the leader of the secular movement. Col. Ingersoll served as President of the American Secular Union and was famous as a freethought orator and essayist. Ingersoll's defense of Charles B. Reynolds against a charge of blasphemy in 1887 was the high water mark of the secular movement in the nineteenth century.

The secular movement was to be in the public focus again early in the twentieth century when the famed attorney Clarence Darrow defended a school teacher in Dayton, Tennessee against the charge of teaching evolution in the classroom. Darrow, like Col. Ingersoll before him, sought to place religion on trial and to preach the virtues of secularism. But, like Col. Ingersoll, Darrow lost the trial. The fact that secular society has generally prevailed in America is attributable, at least in part, to the closing arguments of Col. Ingersoll and Clarence Darrow.

Select Bibliography

Dickinson W. Adams (ed.). *Jefferson's Extracts from the Gospels: "The Philosophy of Jesus" and "The Life and Morals of Jesus"* Princeton, NJ: Princeton University Press (1983)

C. H. Cramer. *Royal Bob: The Life of Robert G. Ingersoll* New York: The Bobbs-Merrill Company, Inc. (1952)

John William Draper. *History of the Conflict Between Religion and Science* New York: D. Appleton and Co. (1875)

Noah Feldman. *Divided by God: America's Church-State Problem* New York: Farrar, Straus and Giroux (2005)

Philip Hamburger. *Separation of Church and State* Cambridge, MA: Harvard University Press (2002)

Robert G. Ingersoll. *Trial of C. B. Reynolds for Blasphemy at Morristown, N.J., May 19th and 20th, 1887* New York: C. P. Farrell (1888)

George E. MacDonald. *Fifty Years of Freethought* 2 vols. New York: Arno Press & The New York Times (1972) [reprint of 1929 ed.]

Samuel P. Putnam. *400 Years of Freethought* New York: The Truth Seeker Company (1894)

Eva Ingersoll Wakefield. *The Letters of Robert G. Ingersoll* Westport, CT: Greenwood Press (1973)

Sidney Warren. *American Freethought 1860-1914* New York: Gordian Press Inc. (1966) [orig. publ. 1943]

Andrew Dickson White. *A History of the Warfare of Science with Theology in Christendom* 2vols. New York: D. Appleton and Co. (1917)

Index

About the Author

Craig Leisy is the author of other self-published volumes including, *The Origins of the Conflict between Science and Religion in Ancient Greece*. In that book, and this one, the historical characters tell the story in their own words. Craig Leisy is currently at work on another project that will examine the evidence of Epicureanism in the life and writings of Omar Khayyam, a medieval Persian mathematician, astronomer and poet, who gained fame after the publication of Edward FitzGerald's translation of the *Rubaiyat of Omar Khayyam* in 1859.

Made in United States
North Haven, CT
11 November 2026

22197194R00068